War and Peace in the Persian Gulf

What Teenagers Want to Know

The Peterson's H.S. Series

Books by, for, and about teens

War and Peace in the Persian Gulf:
What Teenagers Want to Know
(A "Peterson's H.S." Special Report)

Greetings from High School
Teenspeak About Life and Acing High School

150 Ways Teens Can Make a Difference
Strategies for Making a Genuine Contribution

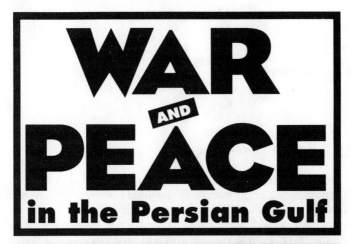

WAR AND PEACE in the Persian Gulf

What Teenagers Want to Know

by Marian Salzman and Ann O'Reilly

with Teresa Reisgies, Terry Barnett,
and several hundred teenage contributors

Peterson's Guides

Princeton, New Jersey

 **Text printed on recycled paper**

Library of Congress Cataloging-in-Publication Data

War and peace in the Persian Gulf : what teenagers want to know : a Peterson's
   H.S. special report / [edited] by Marian Salzman and Ann O'Reilly with Teresa
   Reisgies, Terry Barnett, and several hundred teenage contributors.
         p.   cm.
      Includes bibliographic references.
      Summary: Discusses the Persian Gulf War, including America's involve-
   ment, media coverage, military campaigns, the people, culture, and traditions
   of the Middle East, and where to go for more information.
      ISBN 1-56079-135-7
      1. Iraq-Kuwait Crisis, 1990–   —Juvenile literature. 2. Middle East —
   History — Juvenile literature. [1. Iraq-Kuwait Crisis, 1990–] I. Salzman,
   Marian, 1959–   .
   DS79.72.W37   1991
   956.05'3 — dc20   91-2569

Cover and text design by Frierson + Mee Associates, Inc.
Cover photograph by Eric Bouvet/Gamma-Liaison

Printed in the United States of America

10 9 8 7 6 5 4 3 2 1

For the men and women,
citizens of the planet Earth, who are
risking their lives for peace.

Table of Contents

Preface

For the past six months, we have been in regular contact with literally thousands of teenagers. We communicate with nearly 30,000 of you through our National High School Reporter™ network. Initially, we envisioned the network as a means of communication that would give us insight into your attitudes, feelings, ideas, outlooks, and thoughts . . . but it has evolved into much more than that. (Bill Bell, an insightful *New York Daily News* columnist, recently reported our involvement with the network — specifically, on how we developed it — as "the ultimate chain letter.")

For one thing, we never planned to be talking with you on such a regular basis, but then, who could have predicted that the world would be turned upside down by the situation in the Persian Gulf? As tensions in the Middle East heightened, and as all of you were forced to realize that the world's days of peace might be numbered, we began hearing from our teenage friends across the country about your fears, anxieties, worries — and, most of all, your questions. This special report — *War and Peace in the Persian Gulf: What Teenagers Want to Know* — grew out of what we heard from you. Many of your comments — a.k.a. teenspeak — run within the pages of this book.

The next two books in the "Peterson's H.S." series are *Greetings from High School* and *150 Ways Teens Can Make a Difference*. And we plan other books — and relevant special reports on an as-needed basis — to help you understand what's happening in the world . . . in your own lives, and in your community. The series wants, and needs, your input. Please write to us and join our network of sources. We'd really like to hear your perspective on war, on peace, and on high school in these times. (We promise to write back!) Also, we're considering special reports on a number of topics: the environment, the sixties, world peace. Let us know what else is on your minds.

Feel free to tell us about your life, your school, your friends, how you envision your future, and the advice you have for others who are juggling the challenges of the teenage years.

Marian Salzman
The Bedford Kent Group
156 Fifth Avenue, 8th floor
New York, NY 10010

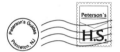

Acknowledgments

This book is a true collaboration between its "creator" and editor, Judy Garodnick, and all of its co-authors: Ann O'Reilly, who commutes to our New York office by fax each day and night and whose input can be found on virtually every page in this book; Teresa Reisgies, an assistant editor at The Bedford Kent Group, who put together the chapters on the environment, how the war has hit home, and military service; and Terry Barnett, who interviewed more than 200 students over three days to find out how they feel about war and peace in the Persian Gulf.

Special thanks to Donna Zaccaro, Cindy Lane Fazio, and Cordelia Richards of The Bedford Kent Group; Gary Goldstein of The Whitney Group; Rick Salomon of Christy & Viener; Peter and Casey Hegener, Wayne Anderson, Paul Mallon, and Meg Palladino of Peterson's Guides; and John Frierson and Heather Mee of Frierson + Mee Associates. Additional thanks to Eric Newman, also of Peterson's Guides, for his dedicated editorial work.

The following schools cooperated with us in the quick compilation of this manuscript by arranging for us to interview their faculty and students:

Agnes Irwin School, Rosemont, Pennsylvania; Alabama Christian Academy, Montgomery, Alabama; Alvarado High School, Alvarado, Texas; Amery High School, Amery, Wisconsin; Andover High School, Bloomfield Hills, Michigan; Archbishop Mitty High School, San Jose, California; Benjamin Franklin Senior High School, New Orleans, Louisiana; The Bishops School, La Jolla, California; Bonanza High School, Las Vegas, Nevada; Brandywine High School, Wilmington, Delaware; Brooks High School, Killen, Alabama; Brunswick School, Greenwich, Connecticut; Burlington High School, Burlington, Vermont; Carthage Senior High School, Carthage, Missouri; Central High School, Columbia, Tennessee; Christian High School, Newark, Delaware; Clayton High School, St. Louis, Missouri; Clearfield High School, Clearfield, Utah; Colonel White High School, Dayton, Ohio; Deerfield High School, Deerfield, Michigan; Denver Christian High School, Denver, Colorado; De Sales High School, Louisville, Kentucky; Dexter Regional High School, Dexter, Maine; East High School, Memphis, Tennessee; Eau Claire Memorial High School, Eau Claire, Wisconsin; Elmhurst High School, Fort Wayne, Indiana; Fairfax High School, Fairfax, Virginia; Fayetteville High School, Fayetteville, West Virginia; Fort Worth Country Day School, Fort Worth, Texas; Franklin County High School, Winchester, Tennessee; Franklin Pierce High School, Tacoma, Washington; Gage Park High School, Chicago, Illinois; Gainesville High School, Gainesville, Florida; George Mason Junior-Senior High School, Falls Church, Virginia; Greencastle-Antrim High School, Greencastle, Pennsylvania; Greensboro Day School, Greensboro, North Carolina; Greenway High School, Phoenix, Arizona; Greenwich High School, Greenwich, Connecticut; Hallandale High School, Hallandale, Florida; Heights School, Potomac, Maryland; Highland High School, Salt Lake City, Utah; Jackson High School, Jackson, Ohio; Lincoln High School, Shinnston, West Virginia; Littleton High School, Littleton, Colorado; Luther High School South, Chicago, Illinois; Marietta High School, Marietta, Georgia; Marlborough School, Los Angeles, California; Millard South High School, Omaha, Nebraska; Mountain Home Junior High School, Mountain Home, Idaho; Nicolet High School, Glendale, Wisconsin; Norcross High School, Norcross, Georgia; North Forsyth High School, Winston-Salem, North Carolina; North Fulton High School, Atlanta, Georgia; Northside High School, Atlanta, Georgia; Overland High School, Aurora, Colorado; Palisades High School, Pacific Palisades, California; Paramus Catholic Boys High School, Paramus, New Jersey; Pascack Valley High School, Hillsdale,

New Jersey; Pilgrim Day School, Los Angeles, California; Pilgrim High School, Warwick, Rhode Island; Reynolds High School, Troutdale, Oregon; River Dell Regional Junior High School, Oradell, New Jersey; Rogers High School, Newport, Rhode Island; Saydel Senior High School, Des Moines, Iowa; Shaker Heights High School, Shaker Heights, Ohio; Springfield High School, Springfield, Vermont; Star Valley High School, Afton, Wyoming; Tempe High School, Tempe, Arizona; T. F. Riggs High School, Pierre, South Dakota; Towson Catholic High School, Towson, Maryland; Tuckerman High School, Tuckerman, Arkansas; University City High School, University City, Missouri; University High School, Morgantown, West Virginia; Upper St. Clair High School, Upper St. Clair, Pennsylvania; Valley Springs High School, Valley Springs, Arkansas; Walt Whitman High School, Bethesda, Maryland; Warren East High School, Bowling Green, Kentucky; and Wellesley High School in Wellesley Hills, Massachusetts.

And we are indebted to the following individuals and organizations that have provided us with information and insights: Carolyn Kolbaba of the American Academy of Pediatrics; Stephen Young and the staff of ACCESS; the Departments of the Air Force, the Army, the Coast Guard, the Marines, and the Navy; Scott Ramey of American Field Service; the American-Israel Public Affairs Committee; the American-Arab Affairs Council; Scott Easton of the American-Arab Anti-Discrimination Committee; Americans for Middle East Understanding; Americans for Peace Now; Arms Control Association; Brookings Institution; Piers Wood of the Center for Defense Information; Cord Brugman of the Central Committee for Conscientious Objectors; Ann Crawford of *Military Living* magazine; the Council on Foreign Relations; Erikson Institute for Advanced Study; the U.S. Department of State; the International Peace Academy; Eric Rozenman of the Jewish Institute for National Security Affairs; Jobs with Peace Campaign; Lawrence Korb of the Brookings Institution; Lee Kravitz of Scholastic, Inc.; Ericka Kurz of the Students' Environmental Action Coalition (SEAC); Joseph Lepgold of Georgetown University; the Mayor's Office of Hinesville, Georgia, and Mayor Homer DeLoach; the Mayor's Office of Virginia Beach, Virginia, Mayor Meyera E. Oberndorf, and Diane C. Roche; the Middle East Institute; the National Association of Arab Americans; the National Peace Institute Foundation; New Israel Fund; Overseas Development Council; Muhammad Hallaj of The Palestine Research and Educational Center; Larry Potter of the Foreign Policy Association; Richard Hobson of the Royal Embassy of Saudi Arabia; Steven Spiegel of the

Department of Political Science at UCLA; John Stroebele; and the United Nations.

From the time that Judy Garodnick approached me with this book idea until I submitted the final manuscript, fourteen days passed. Every effort has been made to ensure accuracy. Also, we have presented as objective an account as is possible and have incorporated the insights and opinions as we were able, given the time limits implicit in a book of this nature and the degree to which reports and opinions conflict. (Because of the sensitive nature of this book's subject matter, most of the teenage participants have been identified by first name only.)

Finally, our thanks to the hundreds of teenagers around the country who shared with us their thoughts and fears and hopes. For the past nine days, we have typed and retyped questions and answers about war and peace and the people in the Gulf. As we learned more and more about the events that have unfolded and about the rich traditions of the region, I have come to realize that there are no black-and-white answers to many of the questions American teenagers have about this conflict. My hope is that this book will motivate its young readers to search for answers to today's conflict and that, in so doing, they will find the key tomorrow's peace.

"Older men declare war.
But it is youth that must fight and die.
And it is youth who must inherit the
tribulation, the sorrow, and the triumphs
that are the aftermath of war."

—*President Herbert Hoover*

"People are going to die, and I just hope
they don't have to reinstate the draft. I just hope
that our country doesn't have to start experiencing
terrorism firsthand. I think that would just
shatter the whole opinion of the war, and divide
the country even more."

—*Peter, a tenth grader from Groton,*
Massachusetts

Introduction

Where Were You When America
Went to War with Iraq?

"At seven o'clock tonight, three o'clock Thursday morning in the gulf, the armed forces of the United States began an operation at the direction of the president to force Saddam Hussein to withdraw his troops from Kuwait and to end his occupation of that country. At the direction of the president, I signed the executive order yesterday afternoon to undertake this operation, subject to certain conditions. It was to begin only after we'd met the terms of the resolution passed last Saturday by the Congress. Those conditions have been complied with, and proper notice has been given, as required. And the operation was not to take place if there had been any last-minute diplomatic breakthroughs. The operation under way tonight, taking place in the pre-dawn darkness of the Persian Gulf, involves allied forces of four nations: the United States, the United Kingdom, Saudi Arabia, and Kuwait.

"As they undertake their missions, they do so after months of careful planning. At the direction of the president, great care has been taken to focus on military targets, to minimize U.S. casualties, and to do everything possible to avoid injury to civilians in Iraq and Kuwait.

"The targets being struck tonight are located throughout Iraq and Kuwait. Our focus is on the destruction of Saddam Hussein's offensive military capabilities — the very capabilities that he used to seize control of Kuwait and that make him a continuing threat to the nations of the Middle East."
—Secretary of Defense Dick Cheney at a news conference in the Pentagon briefing room, January 16, 1991, 9:31 P.M. EST

Where were you when America bombed Iraq? For an entire generation of teenagers, the American bombs that rocked the Middle East shattered a lifetime of peace. For the first time since you were born, America was at war. It was a night you'll never forget. Somehow, the fact that you were at basketball practice, had just come home from school and were playing couch potato in front of the tube, or were sitting at a table in the library and contemplating your physics assignment when you first heard the news will take on a sense of historical importance. Years from now, you'll kick back and say, "I remember the day when we went to war with Iraq. . . ."

For your young brothers and sisters, the war in the Gulf may well become their "earliest memory." I can certainly relate to that. My earliest memory is of the afternoon of November 22, 1963. I was nearly four the day President John F. Kennedy was shot. I also remember watching his funeral procession on television, in my parents' bedroom, a few days later. I can't remember anything about my first day of school, any of my birthday parties, or even the arrival of my first dog, but I'll never forget the sense of childish devastation I felt as I watched President Kennedy's young kids mourn their father. At three years and eight months I no longer felt entirely secure.

For many of today's young people, January 16, 1991, will always be remembered as *the* day. The day we went to war. The day we lost our sense of absolute security, of comforting normalcy. After all, until this conflict your generation had known nothing but peace and prosperity. Many of the high school seniors reading this book were born in 1973, the year the United States signed a cease-fire agreement and withdrew its troops from Vietnam. By the time today's twelfth graders were headed to kindergarten, the landmark Camp David accords (between Israel and Egypt) had been signed, and Soviet Premier Leonid Brezhnev and President Jimmy Carter were well on their way to signing the SALT II Treaty in Vienna.

Who among us could have imagined last spring that within the first month of 1991, the United States would be engaged in an all-out war? Not a "surgical strike" against Libya or a short-lived military action in Panama, but an honest-to-God war, complete with ground assaults, air strikes, POWs, MIAs, and environmental terrorism. Was it only a year ago that the world seemed finally to be heading toward unity — and healing? The Berlin Wall came down in chunks, a symbolic precursor to the reunification of Germany. Revolutions rocked Eastern Europe, bringing hope to millions of oppressed people around the world. And, in the ensuing months, the president of the Soviet Union — a country that not long ago was our most bitter enemy — became an American hero and received the Nobel Peace Prize. How did it end so abruptly? One day, we're celebrating the end of the Cold War; the next day, we're watching American POWs being paraded around by a former ally. No wonder we all feel a little shell-shocked.

> **QUOTE:**
> "THERE WAS NEVER A GOOD WAR OR A BAD PEACE." — *BENJAMIN FRANKLIN*

Life has hit all of us hard these past few weeks. But perhaps it has hit teenagers hardest, because you're the ones most aware of just how precarious — and precious — our way of life is. You're the ones who have been so committed to trying to solve all of our other problems, from AIDS, drug abuse, the destruction of the environment, and homelessness to broken families, deteriorating schools, and urban violence. You're the ones who have worked so hard to make a difference — through community service programs in your high schools or hometowns, and even on a national and international scale.

This past October, Peterson's Guides hosted the National Teenage Summit in New York City. Nearly fifty teenage delegates from thirty states attended; former Democratic vice presidential candidate Geraldine Ferraro was the keynote speaker for the closing session. Guess what the most important questions she fielded were about? If you guessed the situation in the Persian Gulf, you're right. In fact, the delegates were so concerned about events in the Gulf that several of them drafted an open letter to teenagers in Iraq. Meraiah Foley, a tenth grader at Oregon Episcopal School in Portland, read the letter aloud to the press in attendance. It said:

"We have been selected as national representatives of our generation. But we really feel that we are very much like you. We have responsibilities to ourselves, our families, our country, and our earth. As citizens and individuals of the world, we are concerned with violence, poverty, drugs, disease, the environment, education, and world peace. As people, we enjoy having fun, experiencing new things, and meeting new people. We share the same universal emotions; we get angry, sad, excited; we experience happiness and pain. While there are differences, we must identify our similarities. Before we can be united as a world community, we must begin to recognize our similarities and accept our differences."

The teenagers who signed the letter on behalf of the forty-six delegates to the summit were Amanda Abraham (Garden City, New York); Kathryn Alexander (Knoxville, Tennessee); Dan Diman (Milwaukie, Oregon); Meraiah Foley (Portland, Oregon); Alexandra Marrufo (New York, New York); Ron Palmon (Tenafly, New Jersey); Maria Rosel (Wallington, New Jersey); and Jeff Toohig (Garden City, New York).

A sad irony is that I received a letter from Ameen A. Rihani, director of the Baghdad International School in Iraq, on January 17, 1991 — the day after war broke out. The letter had been mailed on December 26, 1990, and was in reference to *Go International!*, a book that will be published by Peterson's Guides as part of its "Peterson's H.S." series. Ironically, the book is intended to help American teens participate more fully in our global community. Ameen Rihani thanked me for inviting his students to participate in the new sourcebook and added, "As you may have noticed, the mail service, to and from Baghdad, is moving at a slow pace, which might interrupt the efficient communication between the students and your office. Anyhow, we'll do our best and hope to be more cooperative and involved in the future."

This letter confirms the conviction that delegates to the National Teenage Summit had when they sent that open letter to their counterparts in Iraq. The delegates recognized that the bonds of humanity are much stronger than the divisive pull of enmity. Whatever one thinks about U.S. and Iraqi policies in the Gulf, the fact that American and Iraqi youths can look beyond their differences to the commonalities of their lives as teenagers should give us all hope that the events of today need not be repeated tomorrow.

Over the past week, Teresa Reisgies, Terry Barnett, Ann O'Reilly, and I have polled more than 200 teenagers to find out what concerns and interests you most about the situation in the Gulf. What follows are answers to some of the basic questions you've told us you have. We've culled through every news report we can get our hands on, talked with spokespeople from the Department of Defense and the State Department, interviewed fifty or sixty Americans in the know — plus more than a hundred American teenagers and fifty more from around the world — in order to bring you the latest on the who, what, when, where, and why of the Persian Gulf.

Marian Salzman
New York, New York
February 18, 1991

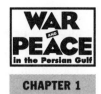
Give Peace a Chance

The Forces of War and Peace

"As long as war is regarded as wicked, it will always have its fascination. When it is looked upon as vulgar, it will cease to be popular."
—Oscar Wilde

Why do we have wars? Aren't there better ways to solve our problems?

War, organized armed conflict between groups of people or states, is an age-old tradition. In fact, war is as old as recorded history itself and most likely goes back even further. The first walled cities known to us were built in approximately 7000 B.C., clearly indicating the need for defense.

But why do people go to war? No other member of the animal kingdom wages war. The reasons for battle most often have to do with power, sovereignty, wealth, territory, security, and ideological domination. These reasons have remained virtually unchanged for the 10,000 years or so that armies have existed. For example, the Messenian Wars (735–461 B.C.) were a series of revolts by Messenia against Spartan domination and expansionism, not unlike the causes of World War II. But what is different today are the consequences of war. Modern wars almost always cost more in terms of human life than is justified by the reasons for conflict. Advanced technology has made it possible for wars to be fought between nations in opposite corners of the world and has given us the capacity to drive ourselves literally to extinction.

Ironically, some people contend that it is this very capacity that will lead us eventually to world peace. They reason that nuclear bombs and other weapons of mass destruction eventually will make war too great a risk for any nation to consider. If we are to avoid being the instruments of our own destruction, we must cease to consider war an option.

What is the role of the United Nations in international peacekeeping, and why hasn't the U.N. been able to keep the world at peace?

"We, the peoples of the United Nations, determined to defend succeeding generations from the scourge of war, which twice in our lifetime has brought untold sorrow to mankind, and to reaffirm faith in fundamental human rights, in the dignity and worth of the human person, in the equal rights of men and women and nations great and small . . . and for those ends to practice tolerance and live together in peace with one another as good neighbors . . . have resolved to combine these efforts to accomplish our aims."
—Charter of the United Nations (1945)

The United Nations was founded immediately after World War II at a conference organized by the "Big Three" Allied powers: the United States, Great Britain, and the Soviet Union. Fifty-one nations signed its charter. The purpose of the U.N. was, and is, to promote peace and international cooperation. It was intended to replace the largely ineffectual League of Nations, which had come out of World War I. The principal organs of the U.N. are the General Assembly (composed of delegates from all member states), the Security Council, the Secretariat, the International Court of Justice, the Trusteeship Council, and the Economic and Social Council.

The Security Council has five permanent members (China, France, Great Britain, the U.S., and the U.S.S.R. — the five greatest Allied powers in World War II) and ten elected members. All of the permanent members of the Security Council have the power of veto, allowing them to prevent the passage of any resolution with which they disagree. Because the members of the Security Council quickly split into two hostile blocs following the establishment of the U.N., the power of veto has effectively prevented the organization from wielding significant power as a world authority. It has been unable to prevent world powers from committing acts of aggression because these nations refuse to submit to an authority over which they don't have total control. Nonetheless, the U.N. is still the primary international body to which nations in conflict can turn, and it has often dispatched peacekeeping forces to sites of conflict at the invitation of the combatants.

The fact that the United Nations authorized the use of force in the Persian Gulf to remove Iraqi troops from Kuwait is significant in that it reflects a radical change within the voting pattern of the Security Council. Former Democratic vice presidential candidate Geraldine Ferraro explains, "Until the invasion by Hussein, the U.N. wasn't looked at as a serious body able to do very much.

> **QUOTE:**
>
> "WHEN KANSAS AND COLORADO HAVE A QUARREL OVER THE WATER IN THE ARKANSAS RIVER THEY DON'T CALL OUT THE NATIONAL GUARD IN EACH STATE AND GO TO WAR OVER IT. THEY BRING A SUIT IN THE SUPREME COURT OF THE UNITED STATES AND ABIDE BY THE DECISION. THERE ISN'T A REASON IN THE WORLD WHY WE CAN'T DO THAT INTERNATIONALLY." —*PRESIDENT HARRY S TRUMAN*

This is because resolutions by the Security Council required a unanimous vote. When we were engaged in the Cold War, the U.S. and the U.S.S.R. always voted against one another. Since the Cold War is over, we are now able to act cooperatively — therefore empowering the United Nations and its Security Council."

Whether the United Nations will ever succeed in its mission to maintain peace in the world will depend on the degree to which its most powerful members cooperate. Only when the world's great powers learn to live in peace will there be a chance that all nations can lay down their arms.

"I wish that the United States didn't have to go through so much red tape with the United Nations. We had definitely reached the point where we had to do something, and I found it frustrating that everything had to be cleared with the U.N. I like the fact that we have allies with us down there, but I think it would be better with just the U.S. fighting. The allies could provide us with the financial support we'd need."—*Jean, a twelfth grader from Wilmington, Delaware*

What is the War Powers Act, and why is it up to Congress to declare war?

There is an ongoing debate in the United States over who (the Congress or the president) has the ultimate authority to commit troops to war. The Constitution grants Congress sole authority to declare war, but it does not specifically forbid the president, as commander-in-chief, from sending troops into action without congressional approval. The result has been a succession of military actions involving U.S. troops that have never been officially declared as wars. Congress has, in fact, declared only five wars: the War of 1812, the Mexican War, the Spanish-American War, World War I, and World War II. In the case of the current war in the Persian Gulf, Congress merely authorized the use of force.

Some members of Congress insist that, in empowering Congress to declare war, the framers of the Constitution intended to prevent the president from sending troops to fight without congressional approval. In 1973, the same year it voted to stop funding the U.S. military action in Vietnam, Congress passed the War Powers Act. It compels the president to notify Congress within forty-eight hours if, without a declaration of war, American troops have been sent into a situation of "eminent hostilities" abroad. It further requires that the president seek formal congressional approval should American troops remain in the area of conflict for more than ninety days.

President Bush, like his predecessors, has refused to recognize the validity of the War Powers Act. However, he asked Congress for a declaration of support before taking offensive military action in the Persian Gulf. On January 12, 1991, the U.S. Congress, by a majority vote, authorized President Bush to use force against Iraq.

What are the Geneva Conventions?

The Geneva Conventions are a series of treaties signed in Geneva, Switzerland, between 1864 and 1949 that provide for the humane treatment of combatants and civilians in wartime.

According to the American Red Cross, the conventions grew out of a plan formulated by Jean Henry Dunant, the Swiss founder of the Red Cross. Horrified by the suffering he saw during the battle of Solferino (Italy) in 1859, Dunant was determined to see that wounded soldiers in future battles received proper treatment.

The first convention, signed by sixteen nations in 1864, concerns the protection of sick and wounded soldiers and medical personnel in land wars. The second convention extends the first to naval warfare. The third covers the treatment of prisoners of war, and the fourth safeguards civilians during wartime.

The International Committee of the Red Cross, a group of twenty-five Swiss citizens, serves as a neutral intermediary between belligerent countries to ensure compliance with the terms of the Geneva Conventions. Although Iraq has committed itself to following the dictates of the conventions, there has been speculation that Saddam Hussein has defied the terms of the third convention during the war against the Allied forces.

What are pacifists and conscientious objectors?

A pacifist believes that violence is never justified, no matter what the cause, and, hence, that peaceful means should always be used to settle disputes. Pacifists generally refuse not only to use force themselves, but also to help others use force: For example, they would not work in a munitions factory. Some American pacifists are Quakers. Their religion — a sect of Christianity — forbids them to fight in wars and even to pay taxes to fund war efforts, although this act would be illegal. Perhaps the best-known pacifist was Mohandas K. Gandhi, the Indian nationalist leader who developed the principle of nonviolent civil disobedience. (Incidentally, Gandhi was one of the heroes named most often when we polled more than 6,000 teenagers in conjunction with another "Peterson's H.S." book, *Greetings from High School*.)

A conscientious objector refuses to bear arms or serve in the armed forces on the basis of moral or religious principles. The Supreme Court has ruled that to be legally considered a conscientious objector, a person must demonstrate a sincere and meaningful belief that occupies a place in his life like that of a more traditional religion. U.S. law makes no distinctions among religious, moral, and ethical beliefs. During World War II, conscientious objectors came from more than 230 religious denominations.

How are the peace protests today different from those held during the war in Vietnam?

Although many of the issues and emotions remain the same, peace protests during the war in the Gulf so far have been markedly different from those held in the '60s and '70s.

QUESTION FOR DISCUSSION:

WHAT DO YOU THINK IS THE MOST EFFECTIVE WAY TO SEND A MESSAGE FOR PEACE TO ELECTED OFFICIALS? DO YOU BELIEVE THAT PEACE PROTESTS ARE HELPING OR HURTING THE CHANCES FOR A QUICK END TO THE WAR IN THE GULF?

Cord Brugman, a staffer at the Central Committee for Conscientious Objectors in Philadelphia, comments, "When you see the peace movement right now, especially when you see televised news reports about the peace movement, you can see immediately how much things have changed since Vietnam. For one thing, there are so many American flags. And today's peace activists have much more credibility — their message is 'Support our troops by bringing them home.' They don't call soldiers 'children killers' as they did during the Vietnam War. There are many Vietnam vets in the peace movement, and they have taught us that the soldiers deserve respect.

"Many of the people who are in the Gulf didn't join the military because they wanted to fight," adds Brugman. "They joined it for job skills, for college money, for adventure, even for travel. . . . It may sound naive that they joined the military without realizing that the ultimate purpose of the military is

FACT:

IT WILL COST KUWAIT AT LEAST $800 MILLION IN THE FIRST THREE MONTHS TO REBUILD ITS ESSENTIAL SERVICES. *(SOURCE: CNN)*

national defense, but there are many men and women in the Gulf today who didn't know that they would ever end up fighting a war. During this war, Americans are very sympathetic to the plight of the soldiers. Their objection is to the war, not to the men and women who are risking their lives every day."

"I don't support U.S. foreign policy at all, but I support the troops," says Meraiah, a tenth grader from Portland, Oregon. "I am totally against war — I don't want to see innocent people get killed. The best way to support the troops is to bring them home alive, and soon."

Is there ever a good reason for a country to go to war? If so, what?

"I think a good reason is if a country is endangering others, and it's also okay if it's legitimate and not just for the sake of being aggressive."—*Eric, a twelfth grader from Salt Lake City, Utah*

"I feel war is necessary if a person is doing something bad to his people, especially if it pertains to their freedom. I feel that the U.S. has had to go in and stop Saddam from invading Kuwait because he had no reason for being there anyway."—*Margaret, a twelfth grader from Las Vegas, Nevada*

"A good reason for a country to go to war is if a country is being taken advantage of and mistreated, such as what is going on in the Persian Gulf. I also think it's important if one person is trying to take over the world, the way Hitler did. Saddam could have been as bad as Hitler if the U.S. didn't stop him."—*David, a tenth grader from Winston-Salem, North Carolina*

"I feel that there is a good reason for one country to go to war with another. That is to gain freedom. I think that war is the only solution if one country can't cooperate with another country for a long period of time; that is, if they can't negotiate peace treaties first."—*Dawn, an eleventh grader from Des Moines, Iowa*

"I feel that the war shouldn't have happened, but I realize that President Bush made the choice that is right for him. I support the troops that are over there, but I want the war to end soon, particularly since my brothers are twenty and I'm scared they'll get drafted."—*Tracey, an eleventh grader from Washington, D.C.*

"I don't think we had a good reason for going to war. I feel that this particular war is only over oil, and I think that there shouldn't have been a deadline for when we'd go to war. We should have given peaceful sanctions a longer time to work. The only reason America should ever go to war is if war is the absolute last solution . . . and nothing else works. If one country invades another and no peaceful treaties can be negotiated, I guess that war has to take place."—*Marcia, a twelfth grader from Dayton, Ohio*

"It's all right for our country to go to war if the nation's best interests are at stake. Every country has to do what's best for itself and its people, but, most important, the people in a country should support the country's leader."
—David, a twelfth grader from Greensboro, North Carolina

"There is no reason for a country to go to war—ever. I'm against war completely. War only results in lives' being lost. In the case of the Persian Gulf, the U.S. is only over there to get oil. I've never believed in war and think that there can always be a peaceful resolution to everything."—Gigi, a twelfth grader from Pacific Palisades, California

QUOTE:

"WAR IS ONLY A COWARDLY ESCAPE FROM THE PROBLEMS OF PEACE." —*THOMAS MANN*

CHAPTER 2

Holy Lands

The History and Peoples of the Middle East

"The Pyramids first, which in Egypt were laid;
Next Babylon's Garden, Amytis made;
Then Mausolos's Tomb of affection and guilt;
Fourth, the Temple of Dian in Ephesus built,
The Colossus of Rhodes, cast in brass, to the Sun;
Sixth, Jupiter's Statue, by Phidias done;
The Pharos of Egypt comes last, we are told,
Or the Palace of Cyprus, cemented with gold."
—Seven Wonders of the Ancient World (Anonymous)

What countries make up the Middle East?

The following are thumbnail sketches of some of the countries in the
Middle East. A map of the region can be found at the end of this chapter.

Bahrain
Area: 240 square miles
Capital: Manama

Government: Traditional monarchy
Population: 481,000
Languages: Arabic, English, Farsi, Urdu
Religions: Shi'ite Muslim (70 percent), Sunni Muslim

Bahrain is one of the more progressive Arab states — the country has a relaxed attitude toward the role of women in society, is liberal in its approach to education, and offers its citizens free health care. The country is an oil producer and refiner, but its reserves have been largely depleted. It is also an international money center. Bahrain is closely allied with Saudi Arabia; a causeway between the two countries provides easy access.

Egypt

Area: 386,900 square miles
Capital: Cairo
Government: Socialist republic
Population: 55 million
Languages: Arabic, English, French
Religions: Muslim (90 percent), Coptic Christian

Egypt became a republic in 1953 and then joined with Syria in the United Arab Republic from 1958 to 1961. Hosni Mubarak became president in 1981 following the assassination of Anwar Sadat. Mubarak has returned Egypt to the center of Arab politics after ten years of isolation caused by Egypt's peace treaty with Israel, which resulted from the Camp David accords. Long dependent on foreign loans and aid, Egypt's economy remains in poor shape.

Iran

Area: 636,296 square miles
Capital: Tehran
Government: Islamic republic
Population: 56 million
Languages: Farsi, Turkish, Kurdish, Arabic, English, French
Religions: Shi'ite Muslim (93 percent), Sunni Muslim, Zorastrian, Jewish, Christian, Baha'i

Originally known as Persia, Iran historically has been at the center of Islamic culture and religion. During the latter part of the Qajar dynasty (1779–1924), Iran was dominated politically and culturally by the European powers, particularly Britain and Russia. The Pahlavi dynasty was founded after World War I. Mohammed Reza Shah Pahlavi, backed by the United States, was driven from Iran by popular opposition in 1979. At that time, the exiled Ayatollah Khomeini, a Shi'ite leader, returned to Iran and established an Islamic republican government.

In November 1979, the U.S. embassy in Tehran was seized by Iranian militants. Over fifty Americans were taken hostage and were not released until 1981. Ayatollah Khomeini was a predominant force in Iranian politics until his death in 1989. During his tenure, Iran fought Iraq in a bloody eight-year war.

Iraq

Area: 167,925 square miles
Capital: Baghdad
Government: Socialist Republic
Population: 18.8 million (80 percent Iraqi Arabs)
Languages: Arabic, Kurdish, Assyrian, Armenian
Religions: Muslim (90 percent, primarily Shi'ite with a Sunni minority); the country's once-sizeable population of Jews has virtually been forced to emigrate to Israel

Contained within Iraq are the fertile plains between the Tigris and Euphrates rivers. Once known as Mesopotamia, the region was home to some of the world's earliest civilizations. The city-states of Sumer were founded in Mesopotamia prior to 3000 B.C.; they later became the heart of the Babylonian Empire. Babylon was conquered by the Persians in the sixth century B.C. and for more than a thousand years remained under the domain of various Persian dynasties.

As the Islamic world expanded in the eighth century A.D., the newly formed city of Baghdad, near the ruins of ancient Babylonia, replaced Damascus as the center of Islam. Baghdad was devastated by Mongol invaders in 1258 and for several hundred years the region fell into decline. In 1533, Baghdad fell to the Ottoman Turks. Iraq remained a province of the Ottoman Empire until the twentieth century.

Britain, which had occupied Iraq during World War I, was allotted the mandate for Iraq in 1920. In 1921, the Hashemite Emir Faisal ibn Hussein was crowned king. Iraq was granted independence in 1932, but Great Britain remained involved in its rule in order to protect British interests in the area. In the late 1940s, Iraq joined the Arab League and the United Nations. Iraqi troops participated in the first Arab-Israeli war, in 1948.

A decade later, the Iraqi monarchy was overthrown in a leftist coup. A republic was proclaimed that summer, and its leaders reversed Iraq's former pro-Western policies. Many of Iraq's industries, including its oil industry, were nationalized. Following the humiliating defeat of the Arabs in the Six-Day War against Israel in 1967, the Nationalist Ba'ath Socialist Party, which had a rival branch in Syria, came to power. Under its leadership, Iraq is ruled by decree, within a republican framework.

Iraq and the U.S.S.R. signed an oil production treaty in 1969 and a treaty of friendship in 1972. The Soviet Union sent Iraq military weapons and advisers and provided important aid during the Iran-Iraq war. Trade relations between Iraq and the West were resumed.

On July 16, 1979, General Saddam Hussein at-Takriti assumed control of the Iraqi government. His first significant action was the purging of Leftist elements from the Ba'ath movement. In 1980 Iraq attacked Iran, beginning an eight-year war between the two countries.

Certain incidents that took place during the Iran-Iraq war helped set the stage for the current war in the Gulf. In 1981, Israel bombed an Iraqi nuclear reactor that they believed to be designed to supply material for nuclear weapons. In 1984, the United States accused Iraq of violating international law by using chemical weapons against Iran. The United Nations supported this allegation.

Israel

Area: 8,019 square miles, excluding occupied territories
Capital: Jerusalem
Government: Parliamentary democracy
Population: 4 million, excluding occupied territories
Languages: Hebrew, Arabic, English
Religions: Jewish (83 percent), Muslim, Christian, Druze

Founded in 1948, Israel is bounded by Lebanon, Syria, Jordan, and Egypt. Nearly 60 percent of Israeli Jews were born in Israel; the remainder are immigrants, mostly from Europe, other countries in the Middle East, North Africa, and the Soviet Union. The great majority of the people in Israel's occupied territories are Palestinian Arabs.

As a result of five major wars with its Arab neighbors and continued threats to its security, Israel has devoted a large percentage of its gross national product to defense expenditures. As a result, its economy has suffered. Israel's current leader is Prime Minister Yitzhak Shamir, a hardliner in terms of policies regarding the Palestinian conflict.

Jordan

Area: 37,738 square miles
Capital: Amman
Government: Constitutional monarchy
Population: 4 million, excluding West Bank
Languages: Arabic, English
Religions: Sunni Muslim (92 percent), Christian

Created by the British after World War I, the emirate of Transjordan became the Kingdom of Jordan in 1946. In 1967, Jordan lost to Israel the area known as the West Bank in the Arab-Israeli War. In 1988, it ceded all claim to that land to the Palestine Liberation Organization (PLO). Jordan's population is now predominantly native Palestinians.

King Hussein has led Jordan since 1953. Of all Arab leaders, he perhaps has been most affected by the war in the Persian Gulf. Deep in debt, Jordan depends on both its economic ties with Iraq and financial aid from the U.S. and Arab states aligned against Saddam in the conflict.

Kuwait (pre–August 2, 1990)

Area: 6,880 square miles
Capital: Kuwait City
Government: Constitutional monarchy
Population: 2 million (60 percent non-Kuwaiti guest workers, mostly Palestinian, Pakistani, and Iranian)
Languages: Arabic, English
Religions: Sunni Muslim, Shi'ite Muslim, Christian, Hindu, Parsi

A major oil producer since the 1940s, Kuwait was a leading economic power at the time of the Iraqi invasion, with an estimated 20 percent of the world's oil reserves. Until the recent conflict, Kuwait had successfully resisted territorial claims by both Saudi Arabia and Iraq.

Since its founding in the eighteenth century, Kuwait has been ruled by the al-Sabah dynasty. The current emir, Sheik Jaber Ahmad al-Sabah, is credited with diversifying Kuwait's economy, and with allowing a degree of political liberalization that stops short of democracy. In the past decade, Sheik Jaber has aligned himself with the moderate Middle Eastern states led by Saudi Arabia. Since the invasion, he has formed a government-in-exile in Saudi Arabia.

Lebanon

Area: 3,950 square miles
Capital: Beirut
Government: Republic
Population: Three million
Languages: Arabic, French, Armenian, English
Religions: Muslim, Druze, Christian

The site of ancient Phoenicia, Lebanon was a French mandate after World War I and was declared independent in 1943. The nation was able to maintain a delicate balance of power between Christians and Muslims, but that balance was upset by an influx of Palestinian refugees, and civil war broke out in 1975. In late 1990, Syria extended its influence over Lebanon, putting an end to the civil war, at least for the time being.

Libya

Area: 679,358 square miles
Capital: Tripoli
Government: People's Republic
Population: 4.2 million
Languages: Arabic
Religions: Muslim

The site of ancient Tripolitania, Libya was under Franco-British rule during World War II. In 1951, the United Nations established Libya as a monarchy, under King Idris I, who developed a policy aimed at the evacuation of all British and U.S. troops stationed in the country. After a coup overthrew the king in 1969, Colonel Muammar al-Qaddafi and a revolutionary council proclaimed Libya a republic. Ten years later, all British and U.S. bases were evacuated, and all oil companies and other economic sectors were nationalized. In 1985, Libya faced serious economic difficulties because of a drop in oil exports. Almost 70,000 foreign workers, mainly Arab, were expelled from the country. A fervent opponent of Israel, Qaddafi has supported a number of international terrorist groups. Attacks by these groups led to the U.S. bombing of Libya in 1986.

Oman

Area: 82,030 square miles
Capital: Muscat
Government: Monarchy

Population: 1.5 million
Languages: Arabic
Religions: Hindu

Oman was converted to Islam in 630 A.D. and remained under Muslim authority until the end of the seventh century. The Kharijite sect of the Ibadiyyah then seized power, and in the ninth century, Oman became an independent imamate. In 1509, the country was conquered by the Portuguese. The sultan of Oman overthrew the Portuguese in 1650 and seized their East African territories to the north of Mozambique. Oman became one of the most important powers in the Indian Ocean during the first half of the nineteenth century. After the conquest of Zanzibar in 1856, the sultan was overthrown and the British imposed a protectorate in 1891.

Disputes with neighboring Saudi Arabia began in 1949, after the discovery of oil fields. Drilling did not begin until 1967. The last British troops pulled out of Oman in 1977. Oman gave its approval to the Camp David agreement by signing a treaty of cooperation with the United States in 1980.

Qatar

Area: 4,416 square miles
Capital: Doha
Government: Traditional monarchy
Population: 414,000
Languages: Arabic, English
Religion: Muslim

Qatar is dominated by its oil industry, one of the richest in the region. A British protectorate from 1916 until its independence in 1971, Qatar has followed a policy of widespread social and economic reform. It shares borders with Saudi Arabia and the United Arab Emirates.

Saudi Arabia

Area: 849,000 square miles
Capital: Riyadh (Mecca is religious capital)
Government: Monarchy
Population: 15 million
Language: Arabic
Religion: Muslim (85 percent Sunni)

Saudi Arabia was never a colony of the European powers, although the

British played an important role in the region until the Kingdom of Saudi Arabia was created in 1932. Saudi Arabia now has the largest oil reserves in the Middle East.

Ruled by King Fahd ibn Abdul Aziz, the Saudi government is dominated by the large royal family. Religious courts, operated under Islamic tenets, are the law of the land. An avowed enemy of Israel, Saudi Arabia normally refuses Jews entry to the country. Exceptions have been made for Jewish members of the Allied forces.

Syria
Area: 71,498 square miles
Capital: Damascus
Government: Constitutional republic
Population: 12.4 million
Languages: Arabic, Kurdish, Armenian, Aramaic, Cicassian, French, English
Religions: Sunni Muslim (90 percent), Alawite, Druze, other Muslim sects, Christian

After gaining independence from Britain in 1944, Syria merged with Egypt to form the United Arab Republic in 1958. Syria became independent again in 1961.

A heavily agricultural country, Syria has close economic ties to the Soviet Union and is bordered by Turkey, Iraq, Jordan, Israel, and Lebanon.

President Hafez al-Assad supported Iran in the Iran-Iraq war and has backed factions within the PLO hostile to the PLO chairman, Yasir Arafat. The ruling Ba'athist Party favors socialism and pan-Arab nationalism. Syria has been linked to international terrorism.

Turkey
Area: 301,382 square miles
Capital: Ankara
Government: Republican parliamentary democracy
Population: 56.5 million
Languages: Turkish, Kurdish, Arabic
Religions: Muslim (98.2 percent, mostly Sunni), Christian, Jewish; religious freedom guaranteed by constitution

Formerly the heart of the Ottoman Empire, Turkey, a non-Arab country, became a republic in 1923. Following World War II, the nation aligned itself with the West and became a member of NATO. President Turgut Ozal is a strong U.S. ally.

Turkey's economy is agriculture-based, and the nation is one of the world's principal producers of chromium.

United Arab Emirates
Area: 32,278 square miles
Capital: Abu Dhabi
Government: Federation of seven Arab states
Population: 1.8 million
Languages: Arabic, Farsi, English, Hindu, Urdu
Religions: Muslim (96 percent), Christian, Hindu

Formerly called the Trucial States, the United Arab Emirates was formed in 1971 and comprises Abu Dhabi, Ajman, Dubai, Fujairah, Ras al-Khaimah, Sharjah, and Umm al-Qaiwain. Dubai has long been the center of Middle East trade.

Oil (from Abu Dhabi, Dubai, and Sharjah) has given the UAE one of the world's highest per capita incomes. Formerly based on herding, oasis agriculture, shipping, and pearl diving, the nation's economy is now dominated by petroleum. Eighty percent of the UAE's labor force is foreign.

Yemen
Area: 203,850 square miles
Capital: San'a
Government: Republic
Population: 9.5 million
Languages: Arabic
Religions: Shi'ite Muslim, Sunni Muslim, Christian, Hindu

Formed in 1990 by the merger of the Yemen Arab Republic and the People's Democratic Republic of Yemen, Yemen is strategically located in the southwestern corner of the Arabian peninsula. Its economy was largely agricultural until oil was discovered there in the 1980s. Shipping is also an important part of the Yemen economy.

Arab Against Arab: Taking Sides in the War in the Gulf

An interview with Steven Spiegel, professor of political science at the University of California at Los Angeles:

Why are some Arab countries fighting against Iraq as part of the Allied coalition? Do you think they'll remain in the coalition for the duration of the war?

Each Arab nation has its own reasons for being in the coalition. Kuwait, Saudi Arabia, and all of the gulf states are very pro-American. On the Egyptian side, the government is pro-American but there are problems with the fundamentalists. Still, I can't see Egypt leaving the coalition unless there are some spectacular developments — such as Israel bombing an Iraqi city or the U.S. killing civilians.

Syria has its own agenda for having joined the allied cause. President Assad is gaining legitimacy and funds. For the first time since the Soviet Union decreased its support, he's back in a strong position. Again, if Israel took a spectacular action, things could change. While there have been problems with the North Africans, Morocco will stick with the coalition unless the U.S. invades Iraq.

Is Iran really neutral?

Iran is antagonistic toward both Iraq and the United States. Neutrality has specific meaning to them. What the Iranians want is for both sides to be defeated. They surely want to see Saddam Hussein bloodied as he bloodied them for years. Yet their fear is that the U.S. has become too powerful in the region. They'll move back and forth, switching sides as it suits them.

How will the Palestinian support of Saddam Hussein affect their cause once the war is over?

The Palestinians are both anti-American and pro-Iraq — a major miscalculation for their cause. If Saddam Hussein is deposed by his people or by American actions, then I would think that there is a possibility of dealing with the

Palestinians. By now the Palestinians should have learned that they cannot depend on outsiders. In the sixties, General Abdel Nasser (president of Egypt from 1956 to 1970) couldn't deliver for them. Then there was Yasir Arafat (chairman of the PLO since 1969). And now they've put their stock into their great savior, Saddam Hussein. If once the war is over, Saddam Hussein is still around, claiming he is a great Arab hero, the Palestinians may still go with him. Factor in that the Israelis have been psychologically traumatized; peace groups in Israel have been hurt; the right-wing groups have been enhanced because they were right — everything they said could happen did. That makes the situation even more tenuous.

There have been attempts to deal with the Palestinian issue: the Camp David Plan, the Shamir Plan, the Reagan Plan. And there will be a further attempt to deal with the Palestinian issue, and that attempt is more likely to succeed if Hussein is out. Washington now believes that there has to be an Arab-Israeli and a Palestinian-Israeli solution. Hopefully, once the war ends there will be series of bilateral dialogues, or some kind of meeting sponsored by the U.S. and U.S.S.R.

What have been the major conflicts in the Middle East during this century?

The history of the Middle East — even its modern history — is complex. But the major milestones that have taken place in that land since the Balfour Declaration declared British Palestine a Jewish homeland are as follows:

1932	• Kingdom of Saudi Arabia decreed by Ibn Saud
	• Iraq gains independence when Britain relinquishes League of Nations mandate
1943	• Lebanon gains independence from France
1944	• Syria gains independence from France
1947	• U.N. announces plan to divide Palestine into a Jewish state and an Arab state. Arabs reject plan.
1948–49	• Israel declared independent state
	• Unsuccessful invasion by Egypt, Iraq, Transjordan (Jordan), Lebanon, and Syria leads to U.N. armistices and additional territory gained by Israel

1950	• Jordan annexes West Bank
1956	• Egypt nationalizes Suez Canal
	• Israel invades Egypt; U.N. ceasefire reached; international forces sent in as peacekeepers
1960	• OPEC formed by Iraq, Iran, Kuwait, Saudi Arabia, and Venezuela
1961	• Kuwait gains independence
	• British troops stop Iraqi attempt to annex Kuwait
1967	• U.N. peacekeeping forces withdraw from Israeli border
	• Egypt closes Gulf of Aqaba to Israeli shipping; Israel defeats Egypt in Six-Day War and gains control of Gaza Strip, Sinai Peninsula, West Bank, Golan Heights, and East Jerusalem
	• Development of U.N. resolution number 242 outlines a plan for peace in the Middle East
1973	• Egypt and Syria attack Israel on Yom Kippur (Jewish Day of Atonement); Egypt and Israel sign cease-fire accord
	• U.N. General Assembly resolution affirms Palestinian right of self-determination and sovereignty within Palestine
1975	• Conflict in Lebanon escalates into civil war
	• Flight from Tel Aviv hijacked to Entebbe, Uganda; Israeli commandos rescue hostages
1978	• Israeli troops attack PLO in Lebanon
1979	• Ayatollah Khomeini establishes Islamic Republic in Iran
	• Egypt and Israel sign Camp David agreement, formally ending hostilities
	• Saddam Hussein becomes president of Iraq
	• Militants occupy U.S. embassy in Iran
1980	• Iran-Iraq war begins
	• Israel annexes Golan Heights; U.N. voids annexation
1982	• Last Israeli troops leave Sinai; five-nation peacekeeping force put in place
	• Israel invades Lebanon
	• Syria sends troops against Israel
	• U.S. Marines enter Lebanon
	• PLO leaves Beirut
1983	• Syria and Lebanon agree to ceasefire
	• Terrorist attack on Israeli headquarters in Lebanon kills sixty
	• U.S. Marine barracks bombed in Beirut

1984	• Marines complete withdrawal from Lebanon
1986	• U.S. bombs Libya
1988	• PLO says it will recognize Israel and renounce terrorism
	• Jordan relinquishes claims to West Bank, declares PLO only legitimate claimant
	• Iraq-Iran war ends
	• Contact established between U.S. and PLO
1990	• Yemen Arab Republic and People's Democratic Republic of Yemen merge
	• Iraq invades Kuwait

> **QUOTE:**
>
> "LET THERE BE NO MORE WAR OR BLOODSHED BETWEEN ARABS AND ISRAELIS. LET THERE BE NO MORE SUFFERING OR DENIAL OF RIGHTS. LET THERE BE NO MORE DESPAIR OR LOSS OF FAITH." —ANWAR AL-SADAT, PRESIDENT OF EGYPT, ON SIGNING THE EGYPTIAN-ISRAELI PEACE TREATY IN 1979

How did Saddam Hussein rise to power?

Saddam Hussein is known worldwide for his extraordinary accomplishments as a terrorist, yet few people can trace his path to power:

Date of Birth: April 7, 1937

1956: Joins the Iraqi branch of the Arab Ba'ath Socialist Party

1959: Saddam flees to Syria and then to Egypt following the failure of a Ba'athist hit man to assassinate Iraqi leader Karim Abdel Kassem

1963: Following the successful assassination of Karim Abdel Kassem, Saddam returns to Baghdad and begins to study law

1964: Saddam is arrested and jailed

1965: While he is still imprisoned, Saddam is elected to leadership in the Ba'ath Party

1968: A bloodless coup — engineered by behind-the-scenes strongman Saddam — brings Ba'ath Party to power in Iraq

1979: Saddam Hussein becomes president of Iraq and initiates repressive policies to ensure his power. According to the *Washington Times* (December 4, 1990), "In his most brutal purge, he ordered the execution of dozens of military officers and party members accused of plotting against him. Hussein videotapes himself smoking a cigar at a large party meeting and reads off the names of coup suspects who are then taken from the room and shot."

1980: Iraq begins an eight-year war against Iran

1988: Turkish refugees report that the Iraqis have been using poison gas against Kurdish civilians in northeastern Iraq

August 2, 1990: Iraq invades Kuwait

(Source: the *Washington Times*, December 4, 1990)

QUESTION FOR DISCUSSION:

RECOGNIZING THAT IT IS PRESENTLY ILLEGAL UNDER U.S. LAW TO ASSASSINATE FOREIGN LEADERS REGARDLESS OF HOW THEY'VE BEHAVED, DO YOU THINK WE HAVE THE RIGHT TO KILL SADDAM HUSSEIN?

What is linkage?

The term *linkage*, in the context of the war in the Gulf, refers to the idea that a resolution of the conflict caused by Iraq's presence in Kuwait should somehow be tied to the resolution of the Israeli-Palestinian conflict. Saddam Hussein has attempted to link the two issues in order to gain support from other Arabs, thereby breaking apart the Allied coalition, and to take attention away from the real issue at hand. He accuses the United States of having a double standard in that the U.S. has taken immediate, strong action against Iraq but has done little to coerce Israel to return the lands that country occupies. Further linking the two issues together, Saddam claims that he would withdraw from Kuwait if Israel were to withdraw from the West Bank. Though it is widely known that President Bush believes that Israel should relinquish the occupied territory on the West Bank, he insists that the issue remain separate from any negotiations between Iraq and the United States.

What caused the Iran-Iraq War?

When Saddam came to power in 1979, he attempted to take advantage of the turmoil in Iran caused by Ayatollah Khomeini's Islamic revolution and possibly topple the Khomeini government. Saddam initiated skirmishes with Iran over control of the contested Shatt-al-Arab waterway (allowing access to the Persian Gulf) and was intent on seizing Iran's oil-rich Khuzistan region. The war that ensued lasted eight years and cost an estimated one million lives.

The war between Iran and Iraq officially started when Saddam Hussein's forces invaded Iran in September 1980. In the 1970s, Iraqi-

Iranian relations were strained when Iran supported the Kurds in their bid for independence from Iraq. The Iraqi Kurdish minority, numbering more than four million, has been fighting since World War II to be declared autonomous. Iraq has violently resisted those demands for self-rule.

What is the Arab League?
The Arab League, or the League of Arab States, promotes broad economic, cultural, and political cooperation among countries in which Arabic culture and language predominate. Founded by Egypt in 1945, the League is made up of twenty sovereign states — Algeria, Bahrain, Djibouti, Egypt, Iraq, Jordan, Kuwait, Lebanon, Libya, Mauritania, Morocco, Oman, Qatar, Saudi Arabia, Somalia, Sudan, Syria, Tunisia, the United Arab Emirates, and Yemen — and the PLO (the Palestine Liberation Organization).

Though Iraq is a member of the Arab League, when the group met on August 10, 1990, for an emergency session, it condemned Iraq's invasion of Kuwait, asserted Kuwait's sovereignty, and agreed to send troops to Saudi Arabia. Two countries — Iraq and Libya — voted against condemning Iraq and sending troops to Saudi Arabia; Tunisia did not attend the meeting because it was not willing to participate in an action that would harm Arab solidarity; and Algeria, Jordan, Mauritania, the PLO, Sudan, and Yemen abstained from voting.

What is the PLO?
The Palestine Liberation Organization was founded in 1964 as a coordinating council for Palestinian refugee groups. Recognized by the U.N. and the Arab states since 1974 as the legitimate government of Palestine, the PLO has as its mission the establishment of a Palestinian state. Though official PLO policy has become more moderate, in the past the group has committed many acts of terrorism. Despite challenges by other factions of the coalition, Al Fatah remains the dominant group in the PLO, and its head, Yasir Arafat, remains chairman.

What is OPEC?
The Organization of Petroleum Exporting Countries (OPEC) was formed in 1960. Its mission has been to coordinate and unify member countries'

petroleum prices and to establish the most appropriate means to protect their interests. Thirteen nations — Algeria, Ecuador, Gabon, Indonesia, Iran, Iraq, Kuwait, Libya, Nigeria, Qatar, Saudi Arabia, United Arab Emirates, and Venezuela — are members of OPEC.

In 1973 and 1979, OPEC's members, acting as a cartel, raised prices sharply, causing oil shortages, inflation, and other problems in the U.S. and other oil-importing nations. Since that time, however, OPEC's power to control oil prices has declined as a result of the growing number of non-OPEC oil producers, the inability of OPEC members to agree on production limits, and worldwide oil conservation measures.

TEENSPEAK:

Do you think there will ever be peace in the Middle East?

"Right now, I feel the only way there ever will be peace is if Saddam is knocked out. I think this particular conflict will be ongoing until Saddam is stopped. As far as the other conflict with Israel and Palestine goes, I don"t think that could ever be resolved. It has been going on for far too long, and it is never ending. So I guess there will never be peace in the Persian Gulf, because of the Israeli-Palestinian conflict."—*Erin, a twelfth grader from Hallandale, Florida*

"I don't think there will ever be peace in the Persian Gulf, because of human nature. First of all, there will never be peace in the Persian Gulf until Saddam is dead. Second, the Israeli and Palestinian conflict will never get resolved, due to their different religions."—*Jeff, an eighth grader from Garden City, New York*

"I think history has proved that there cannot be peace in the Persian Gulf, because of the difference in religion. I think there will always be a conflict in the gulf because if it is not Saddam trying to be powerful it will be someone else. I really think there will never be peace." —*James, a twelfth grader from Fort Wayne, Indiana*

"I think eventually we will be forced to have peace. It may be a while before the conflicts are resolved. As far as the Israel/Palestinian ongoing hatred for

one another goes, I think the Israeli conflict will end in an acceptance. What I mean by this is neither country will have to find a new home. I think people eventually come to tolerate each other, and people learn to accept other people no matter what religion you are. I also believe that the conflict in the Persian Gulf will end. That is definitely not going to last forever. The United States will do what it has to do and then get out of the Persian Gulf."
—*Molly, a twelfth grader from Atlanta, Georgia*

"I don't think in the Middle East there will ever be complete peace. I think the war will be over soon; that is, within three months. I'm hoping the war will end in a peace treaty, but I am sure that this won't happen and it's going to come down to killing Saddam Hussein. I really think there will not be peace in the Middle East for a very long time. Israel and Palestine have not gotten along for so long, and I don't think Israel will give up their land to Palestine. As a result, there cannot be peace in the Middle East."—*Robert, a twelfth grader from Canby, Minnesota*

"I don't think there will ever be peace in the Middle East because of the oil and so many countries involved with it. All the countries will never agree on anything. There are also the religious problems in the Middle East. I feel the physical war will end but there will be ongoing conflicts for one reason or another. If it is not because of the difference in religion then it will be a conflict over oil or some economic reason."—*Rachel, a twelfth grader from Rosemont, Pennsylvania*

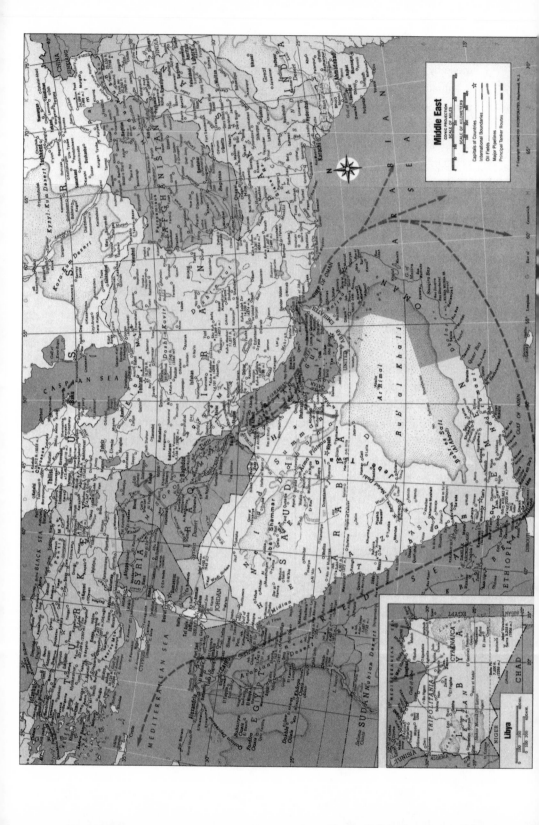

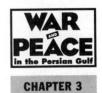
Between Iraq and a Hard Place

The War in the Persian Gulf

"I think this is the next World War II. But a lot of kids don't realize how serious it is yet. After the first day of the war, everyone was like, 'Yeah, we kicked their butts,' but now that it's going on and on and we haven't been as successful as we thought, people don't say as much. I think this war is really going to spread — throughout the Middle East and beyond."

—Jean, a twelfth grader from Wilmington, Delaware

What events led to the Iraqi invasion of Kuwait?

Tensions between Iraq and Kuwait existed long before Saddam's invasion of Kuwait on August 2, 1990. For decades Iraq has made territorial claims against the emirate and has been particularly intent on gaining increased access to the Persian Gulf. Iraq acknowledged Kuwait's sovereignty in 1963, yet in 1973 Iraq initiated border skirmishes with Kuwait over the islands of Warbad and Bublyan. The islands remained under Kuwaiti control.

Despite Kuwait's political and economic support of Iraq during the Iran-Iraq War (1980–88), Saddam became increasingly hostile toward Kuwait in 1990. On July 16 — precisely six months before the initial U.S. bombing of Iraq — Saddam accused Kuwait of stealing $2.4 million worth of Iraqi oil from the Rumaila oil field, which straddles the border between the two countries. The next day he threatened to use force against Kuwait and the United Arab Emirates if they didn't stop what he considered to be the overproduction of oil. During an OPEC meeting later that month, Kuwait and the United Arab Emirates agreed to cut their oil output by 1.5 million barrels a day. This concession failed to appease Saddam. He continued to amass troops on the border with Kuwait until they numbered 100,000.

On July 31, delegates from Iraq and Kuwait met in Saudi Arabia to negotiate their oil and border dispute. The talks broke down the following day, and the land border between the two countries was closed. A day later, Iraq invaded Kuwait and occupied its capital.

What steps did the Allied coalition take prior to January 16 to compel Saddam to withdraw from Kuwait? What was the Iraqi response?

The following timeline lists the major events that took place from the invasion of Kuwait to the onset of Operation Desert Storm.

August 2 Iraq invades Kuwait; within seven hours, troops occupy the capital. Kuwait's ambassador to the United States says Iraqi troops are moving toward the southern part of the country, near the border with Saudi Arabia. The United States, France, and Britain call for the immediate withdrawal of Iraqi troops from Kuwait, freeze Iraqi and Kuwaiti assets, and stop arms deliveries to Iraq. The Soviet Union, Iraq's chief arms supplier, announces a halt of arms sales to Baghdad. The U.N. Security Council, in an emergency meeting, passes Resolution 660, which condemns Iraq's invasion and demands its immediate withdrawal.

August 3 In a joint statement, Soviet Foreign Minister Eduard Shevardnadze and U.S. Secretary of State James Baker call for the unconditional withdrawal of Iraqi troops from Kuwait and the restoration of the emirate's sovereignty. They also urge the international community to halt arms deliveries to Iraq. President Bush says he would favor U.S. military support of Saudi Arabia if that country were attacked by Iraq. Washington asks Turkey and Saudi Arabia to close the Iraqi oil pipeline running through their territories. The ministerial council of the League of Arab States meets in Cairo and urges an Arab solution to the crisis; in a 12-to-9 vote, it condemns the invasion, calls for Iraq to withdraw from Kuwait, and warns against foreign intervention in any Arab country.

August 4 The European Community freezes Iraqi and Kuwaiti assets.

August 5 President Bush says he will not accept anything less than a total Iraqi withdrawal from Kuwait.

August 6–7 Iraqi troops round up hundreds of Westerners in Kuwait. President Bush launches "Operation Desert Shield," ordering U.S. warplanes and several thousand troops to Saudi Arabia and the Persian Gulf. The U.S.S.R., Britain, and France also send ships to the Persian Gulf. The U.N. Security Council approves Resolution 661, prohibiting all U.N. members from buying oil or having virtually any other commercial or financial dealings with Iraq and Kuwait.

August 8 Iraq formally annexes Kuwait and declares that all foreign missions in the capital must move their staffs to Baghdad. President Bush defines U.S. policy objectives: unconditional Iraqi withdrawal, restoration of the legitimate government of Kuwait, maintenance of security in the Persian Gulf, and protection of U.S. citizens. Washington calls for a "multinational" force to join the 4,000 U.S. troops now deployed in Saudi Arabia. The Soviet Union says it will join a U.N. force in the Gulf.

August 9 U.N. Security Council Resolution 662 unanimously condemns Iraq's invasion of Kuwait and declares its annexation of Kuwait "illegal." Iraq closes its borders and announces that foreign nationals in Iraq and Kuwait will not be permitted to leave.

August 10 At an emergency meeting, the Arab League votes to condemn Iraq's aggression against Kuwait and to assert Kuwait's sovereignty; it also agrees to send troops to Saudi Arabia. The vote is sharply divided. Saddam Hussein calls for a "holy war" to liberate Islam's holy sites.

August 11 Egyptian troops are deployed to Saudi Arabia. Thousands of Jordanians and Palestinians demonstrate against U.S. intervention; nearly 80,000 say they would fight on the side of Iraq.

August 12 Saddam Hussein offers a "peace plan" to resolve "all issues of occupation" in the Middle East, including Israeli withdrawal from the occupied territories and Syrian withdrawal from Lebanon. The Bush administration rejects any linkage between the situations. Bush says that the United States will use force to stop any ships trying to break the U.N. embargo.

August 15 King Hussein of Jordan meets with Bush, who indicates that he will provide Jordan with more economic aid if it supports the embargo and closes off the port of Aqaba to Iraq. U.S. strength in the Gulf now totals about 60,000 troops.

August 16 King Hussein of Jordan assures President Bush that Jordan will close Aqaba to most Iraqi commerce but insists that the embargo does not include food and medical supplies. Iraq orders 4,000 Britons and 2,500 Americans in Kuwait to assemble in Kuwaiti hotels.

August 18 Iraq announces that citizens of "aggressive nations" held in Kuwait and Iraq (excluding Egyptians) have been moved to strategic military and civilian installations. The U.N. Security Council unanimously passes Resolution 664, calling for Iraq to release foreign nationals detained in Iraq and Kuwait.

August 19 Saddam Hussein offers to let Westerners leave Iraq and Kuwait if President Bush pledges to withdraw all U.S. troops from the region and lift the embargo, and that any such agreement must be backed by a U.N. Security Council guarantee that U.S. forces leave according to a fixed timetable. Also, Iraq and Saudi Arabia must agree not to attack the other.

August 22 For the first time since the Vietnam era, President Bush summons military reservists to active duty. The initial request involves 49,700 reservists. Jordan's King Hussein announces that he will visit Iraq and other Arab countries in a "last effort" to end the standoff peaceably. Crude oil tops $30 a barrel in U.S. trading, the highest price since 1985.

August 23 Jordan, overwhelmed by nearly 200,000 refugees from Iraq and Kuwait, temporarily closes its borders with Iraq. Palestine Liberation Organization leader Yasir Arafat and other PLO diplomats continue efforts to resolve the crisis within the Arab world, visting leaders in several Arab states.

August 24 Iraqi troops surround at least eight embassies in Kuwait that have defied the Iraqi order to shut down. Iraq announces that it will withdraw diplomatic immunity of male diplomats whose countries refuse to close their missions but will free their dependents.

August 25 The U.N. Security Council passes Resolution 665, implicitly authorizing the use of military force ("necessary measures") as a means of enforcing economic sanctions against Iraq. Iraqi troops continue to round up foreigners and cut off water and electricity to some diplomatic missions in Kuwait.

August 29 With Iraq, Iran, and Libya dissenting, OPEC ministers in Vienna decide to temporarily increase crude oil production by four million barrels a day. Iraq announces that foreign women and children may seek exit visas and leave the country. Iraq's ambassador to Washington says that male foreigners may leave if the United States promises not to launch a military strike.

August 30 President Bush indicates that Washington is considering forgiving Egypt's $7.1 billion military debt to the United States. Only twelve of the twenty-one Arab foreign ministers attend the first day of the Arab League meeting in Cairo; the League is basically split into two camps, one generally supporting U.S. action (Bahrain, Djibouti, Egypt, Kuwait, Lebanon, Morocco, Oman, Qatar, Saudi Arabia, Somalia, Syria, and the United Arab Emirates) and the other opposing Western intervention

(Algeria, Iraq, Jordan, Libya, Mauritania, the PLO, Sudan, Tunisia, and Yemen).

August 31 U.N. Secretary-General Javier Perez de Cuellar and Iraqi Foreign Minister Tariq Aziz meet; de Cuellar characterizes the meetings as both a failure and "the beginning of a process." Thirteen Arab League members attending the Arab League meeting in Cairo adopt tough resolutions against Iraq, demanding unconditional withdrawal from Kuwait and the payment of war reparations.

September 26 The U.N. Security Council expands the embargo against Iraq and Kuwait to include air traffic (Resolution 670), barring passenger and cargo traffic except in humanitarian circumstances.

October 3 The U.S. Senate, by a 96-to-3 vote, approves a resolution supporting deployment of U.S. military troops to the Gulf.

October 5 The *Washington Post* reports that the Gulf buildup has reached 200,000 U.S. troops and almost 100,000 troops from other nations.

October 20 The first large U.S. protests against a U.S. military presence in the Persian Gulf take place, demanding that U.S. troops be brought home immediately.

October 29 The U.N. Security Council passes Resolution 674, demanding that Iraq cease detaining foreign nationals.

November 8 Stating the need for an "offensive option," President Bush announces that the United States will commit up to 200,000 additional troops to the Persian Gulf, bringing U.S. troop levels to 430,000 by February.

November 20 Congressman Ron Dellums (D., Ca.), along with fifty-two other representatives and one senator, files suit in Federal District Court seeking an injunction to prevent President Bush from going to war in the Persian Gulf without congressional approval. The judge subsequently refuses to grant an injunction but allows that such an injunction is possible if the full Congress seeks it.

November 22 President Bush, in Saudi Arabia visiting U.S. troops on Thanksgiving, states that Iraq's nuclear weapon potential adds "a real sense of urgency" to the mission of U.S. troops.

November 29 The U.N. Security Council adopts Resolution 678, authorizing the use of force ("all necessary means") if Iraq does not comply with previous Security Council resolutions. The resolution gives Iraq until January 15, 1991, to comply.

November 30 President Bush, for the first time, offers to talk with Iraq on the Persian Gulf crisis and suggests a meeting between U.S. Secretary of State Baker and Saddam Hussein.

December 6 Saddam Hussein announces that all hostages and foreigners in Iraq and Kuwait can leave.

December 11 U.S. citizens in Iraq and Kuwait are permitted to leave.

December 18 A tentative meeting between President Bush and Iraqi Foreign Minister Tariq Aziz is indefinitely postponed because the two sides cannot agree on a reciprocal visit by U.S. Secretary of State Baker to Iraq.

December 19 American troops and Allied forces will not be ready to attack on the January 15 deadline set by the U.N. Security Council, according to Lieutenant General Calvin Waller, deputy commander of the American forces in the Gulf.

January 2, 1991 NATO sends forty-two aircraft to Turkey to protect that nation from possible attack by Iraq.

January 9 U.S. Secretary of State Baker and Iraqi Foreign Minister Aziz meet in Geneva but fail to make any progress. President Bush characterizes the Iraqi position as "a total stiff-arm."

January 10 The U.S. Congress begins hearings on authorizing President Bush to use force against Iraq but does not yet debate a declaration of war. Almost all Western embassies in Baghdad are shut down.

January 12 Without issuing a declaration of war as such, the U.S. Senate, by a vote of 52–47, and the House of Representatives, by a vote of 250–183, authorize President Bush to use force against Iraq.

January 13 Achieving no progress in meetings with Saddam Hussein, U.N. Secretary-General Perez de Cuellar says "only God knows" if there will be war.

January 15 France, in a last-ditch effort to prevent war, proposes that the U.N. Security Council agree to an international conference on the Palestinian situation if Iraq withdraws from Kuwait. The United States and Great Britain strongly oppose the proposal. The U.N.-established midnight deadline for Iraqi withdrawal from Kuwait passes; Iraq makes no move to comply with the U.N. Resolutions.

(Sources: the *New York Times*, the *Washington Post*, *Middle East Report*, and *Israel & Palestine Political Report*, excerpted from a compilation by ACCESS: A Security Information Service)

Why didn't President Bush give the sanctions against Iraq more time to work?

According to the State Department's Office of Public Liaison, Bureau of Public Affairs, President Bush was convinced that continued sanctions alone would not force Saddam Hussein out of Kuwait. In fact, the prevailing wisdom among Americans in the know was that the longer Saddam was allowed to remain in Kuwait, the more difficult it would be to drive him out.

Proponents of swift military action cited five primary concerns: (1) that Saddam would continue to plunder Kuwait and pose a threat to its citizens; (2) that Saddam would fortify Kuwait, making an Allied invasion much more difficult; (3) that Saddam would use the gained time to stockpile chemical and biological weapons; (4) that Saddam would manage to acquire nuclear capability; and (5) that Saddam would bring out other issues designed to dissolve the coalition arrayed against him.

SPOTLIGHT:

A Mission in Diplomacy: Six Months in the Life of James Baker, August 2, 1990, to January 15, 1991

Summary
- More than 200 contacts with foreign dignitaries (bilateral meetings, events)
- Six congressional appearances
- 103,421 miles traveled

Trips

1990
- August 3: Moscow
- August 8–10: Ankara, Brussels (NATO)
- September 5–15: Jeddah, Taif, Abu Dhabi, Cairo, Alexandria, Helsinki, Brussels, Moscow, Damascus, Rome, Bonn
- September 26–October 5: New York (United Nations and CSCE ministerial)
- November 3–10: Manama, Dhahran, Taif, Jeddah, Cairo, Ankara, Moscow, London, Paris
- November 15–26: Brussels, Geneva, Paris, Jedda, San'a, Bogota
- November 28–29: New York (U.N.)
- December 9–12: Houston (U.S.–U.S.S.R. ministerial)
- December 16–18: Brussels (NATO)

1991
- January 6–14: London, Paris, Bonn, Milan, Geneva, Riyadh, Abu Dhabi, Taif, Cairo, Damascus, Ankara, Ottawa

Meetings
Secretary Baker has held more than 200 meetings since August 2, 1990, with:
- Soviet officials (thirty-five meetings)
- Representatives of every NATO member (fifteen nations)
- CSCE signatories (thirty-three nations)
- All Gulf nations except Iran
- Cuba (which, with Yemen, voted against U.N. Resolution 678, authorizing the use of force)

Which countries make up the Allied coalition? What have they contributed to the Allied effort?

The following countries make up the anti-Iraq coalition, although only a handful are actively involved in supporting fighting troops. They are Argentina, Australia, Bahrain, Bangladesh, Belgium, Canada, Czechoslovakia, Denmark, Egypt, France, Germany, Greece, Italy, Kuwait, Morocco, the Netherlands, Niger, Norway, Oman, Pakistan, Poland, Qatar, Saudi Arabia, Senegal, Spain, Syria, United Arab Emirates, United Kingdom, and the United States. The Associated Press reports that as of January 16, 1991, there are a total of 648,000 Allied troops stationed in the Gulf. The breakdown is as follows: U.S. 425,000; Saudi Arabia and other Arab Gulf states 150,500; Britain 35,000; France 10,000; Egypt 38,500; Syria 21,000; and Pakistan 13,000. That compares with an Iraqi force of 545,000 in occupied Kuwait and southern Iraq and 490,000 elsewhere in Iraq.

In addition, more than fifty countries have committed financial support to the Allied effort in the Gulf. Secretary of State James Baker has indicated that the U.S. expects its coalition partners to finance approximately 80 percent of the cost of the war in the first quarter of 1991. Budget director Richard Darman announced on February 5, 1991, that Allied countries had pledged a total of $51.5 billion in cash and contributions of equipment and fuel. "The pledges are a very, very substantial portion of the actual costs incurred," he said. In conjunction with Allied financial support of the war, President Bush stated, "There has never been a clearer demonstration of a world united against appeasement and aggression."

Funding of Operation Desert Shield

Nation	Amount Pledged (millions)	Amount Received (millions)
Kuwait	$2,500	$2,500
Saudi Arabia	Open-ended	987
Japan	2,000	476
Germany	1,072	337
United Arab Emirates	1,000	280
South Korea	95	4
Foreign Contributions	6,667	4,584

Estimated cost of Desert Shield through January 1, 1991: $10 billion

Estimated cost of a one-month war: $60 billion

(Source: *Fortune*, February 11, 1991)

What's the breakdown of U.S. forces in the Gulf in terms of branch of service?

Pete Williams, spokesperson for the Office of the Assistant Secretary of Defense, says that as of the afternoon of January 31, 1991, just over half a million U.S. troops were deployed in the Gulf. He breaks it down as follows: 280,000 Army; 80,000 Navy; 50,000 Air Force; 90,000 Marines. "Those are rough figures," says Williams. "Not all those people are with Army units — some of them are support units in Riyadh."

There are now 207,313 members of the National Guard and the reserves in the Gulf, according to Williams. "That's 143,067 for the Army; 15,182 for the Navy; 25,813 for the Air Force; 22,472 for the Marine Corps; and 779 for the Coast Guard."

Troops stationed in the Persian Gulf account for approximately 12 percent of total U.S. forces around the world, including reserves.

Why aren't Saudi Arabian and Kuwaiti forces doing most of the fighting? What contributions have they made to the Allied effort?

Saudi Arabia and Kuwait, which have long been peaceful countries, simply don't have the military muscle to take on Saddam Hussein. Iraq has the fourth-largest military in the world.

The media have also reported that the U.S. has placed restraints on Kuwaiti military action in the Gulf. According to *Time* (February 4, 1991), "Pentagon planners are resisting pressure from the Kuwaiti royal family to include Kuwaiti troops in the first wave of any group attack to free their country. U.S. officials fear that the returning Kuwaitis might slaughter every Palestinian in sight. Many of the exiles believe that Palestinians living in the emirate collaborated with the Iraqi army and revealed information about important Kuwaitis to the invading forces. Pentagon officials prefer to place Saudi troops, instead, in the vanguard of any assault."

What the Saudis and Kuwaitis have been unable to provide in terms of military muscle has been made up by their significant financial contributions. For the period from January 1 through March 31, 1991, the Kuwaitis and Saudis have each pledged $13.5 billion.

QUESTION FOR DISCUSSION:

DO YOU THINK THAT AMERICANS SHOULD PAY A SPECIAL TAX TO COVER WAR COSTS?

SPOTLIGHT:

The Weapons of War

We spoke with Piers Wood, chief of staff of the Center for Defense Information in Washington, D.C. He is a lieutenant colonel in the U.S. Army reserves, a veteran of combat in the Vietnam War, and a graduate of West Point.

What kinds of weapons does Saddam Hussein have?

FACT:

ALTHOUGH AFRICAN-AMERICANS MAKE UP 12 PERCENT OF THE U.S. POPULATION, THEY REPRESENT 25 PERCENT OF THE FIGHTING FORCES IN THE PERSIAN GULF. ACCORDING TO A *TIME*/CNN POLL TAKEN IN LATE JANUARY 1991, 49 PERCENT OF ALL BLACKS SUPPORTED INVOLVEMENT IN THE WAR IN THE GULF, COMPARED WITH 77 PERCENT OF WHITES.

The Iraqis have some high-quality tanks, but the large majority of what they have are Vietnam-era tanks. Saddam Hussein has got a good late-seventies, early-eighties arsenal. In comparison, we have a good nineties arsenal and certain high-tech advances that Hussein can't possibly compete with.

Do you believe that Saddam Hussein will use biological or chemical weapons?

I really don't. While Saddam Hussein himself doesn't have to fear military retaliation, the Iraqis won't use biological or chemical warfare, because, if they did, the Allied troops would retaliate in devastating ways — and Hussein knows this. Actually, more than fear of retaliation, the reason Hussein will forgo the use of these weapons is that they are not militarily effective. There is a great deal of trouble and risk involved in using biological and chemical weapons. They're a terror weapon — they create panic but in the end do not inflict the casualties that make them worth it.

What exactly are the "nineties" weapons America has?

Our weaponry is state of the art and includes: (1) the ability to disseminate satellite intelligence down to the tactical (or local) level — today the guy who shoots the cannon is able to use satellite imagery; (2) very practical night-vision capability, which is a wonderful advantage (in comparison, Saddam Hussein's night vision is equivalent to what we had in Vietnam); (3) electronic warfare that is able to blind temporarily, as we did the first night we went into Baghdad; (4) "smart" munitions — weapons that are independently guided in the terminal phase using electronic beams, lasers, and television to ensure that they hit their targets; (5) global positioning — that is, satellites that can be used to locate instruments on the ground, and with great precision; and (6) the added mobility of the M-1 tanks — they can now travel at thirty miles an hour and can fire as they're moving. These and the Bradley fighting vehicle, a lightly armored personnel carrier, give us wonderful mobility.

How do you think that the war will end?

Our great fear at the Center for Defense Information is that America will not utilize its technological advantage, that we'll launch a frontal offense. A ground assault could be skipped. We think that the Allied forces should let Saddam Hussein bleed to death under an embargo blockade, capitalizing on our air supremacy. Sure, it may take until next August [1991] to actually win, but it would save 45,000 casualties — and 10,000 soldiers' lives.

What is the "elite" Republican Guard?

Ever since the outbreak of war in the Gulf, the U.S. media have been reporting on Pentagon efforts to neutralize Saddam's Republican Guard. Massive air strikes have been made against the Guard since the second day of Operation Desert Storm.

The 100,000-member Republican Guard are Iraq's best-trained and best-equipped fighting forces. Approximately one-fifth of the Iraqi army, members of the Guard make twice as much as ordinary soldiers and are given other perks such as free housing and cars.

Saddam originally used members of the Guard as bodyguards, but during the war against Iran he turned them into a military force. They were highly successful in that war and reportedly became expert at the use of chemical weapons.

The extent to which Allied forces have been able to neutralize the Guard is not certain. Reports indicate that the majority of the Guard's divisions are deployed along Kuwait's northern border with Iraq. One division remains in Baghdad to protect Saddam and other members of the Iraqi government.

Why is Saddam Hussein commonly referred to by his first name rather than his surname?

Saddam Hussein reportedly prefers to be known by his first name because his last name, which refers to the grandson of the prophet Mohammed, is one of the most common in the Middle East. The use of "Saddam" also prevents confusion with King Hussein, the leader of neighboring Jordan.

TEENSPEAK:

Do you support President Bush's actions in the Persian Gulf?

"I completely support President Bush's actions. He is helping Kuwait because Saddam should not have been there in the first place. Saddam was completely wrong to try and ruin the environment and now he is doing all these terrible terrorist acts. I think that the U.S. should be there." —*Jason, a twelfth grader from Warwick, Rhode Island*

"Since the efforts for peace didn't work with Iraq, I feel that the U.S. had to go in and stop Saddam. Force is the only way to stop him."—*Vanessa, a ninth grader from Nashville, Tennessee*

"I don't agree with President Bush's actions, because I feel there could have been other ways to solve the problem. Bush did not leave Saddam any way to get out of the situation. Saddam has pride and Bush knew that. Bush could have given him a partial agreement. But now that we're over there, I think we have to stop Saddam. We must destroy him."—*Zeke, a twelfth grader from Tuckerman, Arkansas*

"I support President Bush completely. I feel that perhaps he knows more information compared to what the rest of America knows. He decided to act before Saddam got a chance to really take over. And Saddam Hussein needed to be stopped before he could use nuclear weapons."—*April, a twelfth grader from Shinnston, West Virginia*

"My feelings are that if the war is being fought to liberate Kuwait it is a good cause. But if it is being fought for oil, we should not be over there."—*Patricia, a tenth grader from Towson, Maryland*

"I support President Bush because I feel that if we are able to get things such as oil from another country, then we should help when military action is needed. We had to help the Kuwaitis stop Saddam because there was no way their small country could do it themselves."—*Brian, a twelfth grader from Omaha, Nebraska*

"I support President Bush because I think that Saddam was wrong and we had to stop him. Bush gave Saddam a proposal and then he had to follow through with it. Still I don't think we gave Iraq enough time and tried hard enough to get a peace treaty."—*Shayne, a twelfth grader from Amery, Wisconsin*

TEENSPEAK LONG DISTANCE:

How do you feel about the war in the Persian Gulf?

"The war annoys me greatly. I don't know if it should be going on, because of all the bloodshed and the pollution. I am very angry at Saddam because he has no right doing what he is doing—he's barbaric and disgusting. I think the U.S. has the right to go in and fight."—*Elliott, a tenth grader from Thames, Oxfordshire, England*

"I don't approve of this war because I don't approve of how the POWs are being treated. I think, though, that America had to go there. Saddam has to

be stopped, and it was up to America to stop him. Saddam is so selfish —
worse than Hitler, even. I think that the U.S. is the right country to have taken
charge and they have the right people to be doing it. I think George Bush is
doing great."—*Laura, a tenth grader from Thames, Oxfordshire, England*

"I feel that the U.S. had to go in and stop Saddam. I blame Saddam for
everything. He is worse than Hitler. He is the most selfish man."—*Rachel, a
tenth grader from Thames, Oxfordshire, England*

"The radio is our main source of news, and I have to say that while kids at my
school are not too upset about the war, many of my friends are Japanese and
they are worried because Japan is spending so much money on the war."
—*Hiroko (Japanese), an eleventh grader from Düsseldorf, Germany*

"At my school, the war is the number one topic, and at the beginning students
worried about what was going on. Every day, for three weeks straight, we got
bomb threats. We followed the news by watching CNN and reading the
International Herald Tribune. At first the kids in our school were looking down
on the French because the French appeared to want to make amends with
Iraq. But [French president François] Mitterrand is so popular here that
everyone was behind him . . . while the French view was that anything was
better than war, people have come behind his policies. Once the war began,
everyone started to get more on the side of the allies.

"In the beginning, people said that Saddam was in there for his old land. I
don't think that Saddam is supported by lots of Europeans. The Iraqi kids who
go to my school have never really lived in Iraq — their parents work in international finance — and for this reason their attitudes are more like the attitudes
of Americans than you'd expect.

"I don't think that the U.S. is in Kuwait for economic reasons. Rather,
we're there to protect international human rights. Saddam Hussein is just
brutal.

"Socially, it was very difficult for me when the war first broke out because
other people would tell me that President Bush had gone to war for the oil."
—*Morgan (American), a twelfth grader from Paris, France*

"At first, we were really scared about the war. We didn't know what it was all
about, but now Israel is a lot more calm. At the beginning, there was no
school for an entire week. We have started back now. We have our classes in

sealed rooms and have to carry our gas masks around with us at all times. About two months before the war began, my school showed films on the use of gas masks. They taught us how to use them. In fact, kids in Israel know better how to use gas masks than our own parents do.

"The last few days, things have been going normal here, except the worst thing is how scared the younger kids are. They don't understand the war, and they're confined to their houses — they can't play outside.

"I'm pleased with what the U.S. has done, but I think that they could be more centered. What I mean by this is that the United States should be even more aggressive by putting pressure on Saddam Hussein — by starting the ground war."—*Ron, an eighth grader from Savyon, Israel*

SPOTLIGHT:
War Talk

Air Force: The branch of the armed services responsible for military operations in the air.

Army: The branch of the armed services responsible for land operations.

Blockade: A military act designed to obstruct the flow of trade, communication, and supplies to an enemy.

Bounty: A reward designed to induce volunteers to enter the armed services.

Carpet Bombing: Dropping large numbers of bombs on a small area.

Casualty: A soldier who is killed, wounded, captured, or missing in action during a war.

Contraband: Goods that are prohibited by law but imported illegally.

Draft: A system of selecting people for compulsory military service.

Embargo: A government order to prevent certain merchant ships from entering or leaving a foreign port.

Espionage: The practice of spying upon a foreign country to gather information for political or military uses.

Joint Chiefs of Staff: A group of military advisers comprising a chairman and the head of each service branch.

Marines: A highly trained branch of the armed services that specializes in combat situations.

Mercenaries: Soldiers who join, merely for wages, the military of a country other than their own.

Military Discharge: A formal release from duty.

Militia: An army composed of ordinary citizens rather than professional soldiers.

National Security: A term used in conjunction with issues involving a country's safety.

Navy: The branch of the armed services responsible for sea-based operations.

Neutral: Not taking sides in a dispute.

Propaganda: Ideas or rumors deliberately spread to promote one's cause or damage an opposing cause.

SAM: Surface-to-air missile.

Sortie: One mission by a single plane.

Truce: A suspension of fighting.

Veteran: A former member of the armed services.

Vital Interest: A policy or goal deemed essential to a nation's well-being.

Source: Excerpted from *Scholastic Update* (February 8, 1991)

SPOTLIGHT:

Persian Gulfspeak

As is the case in every war, the Persian Gulf conflict has spawned its own slang, euphemisms, and acronyms. A few examples follow.

BDAs ("Bomb damage assessments"): detailed analyses of the air war's effectiveness

Big Red: the desert sun

Bird: helicopter from which paratroopers jump

Chocolate chips: desert camouflage uniforms

Collateral Damage: civilian casualties

Droe: remote-controlled planes that fly above a battle zone and send back pictures of enemy troops

KSA: Kingdom of Saudi Arabia

MRE ("Meal Ready-to-Eat"): plastic-wrapped, pre-prepared food served to the forces

Patriot: missile that explodes near its target, destroying it with shrapnel

Scud: Russian-made surface-to-air missile

"Smart" bombs: bombs guided to targets by laser beams

Wadi: a deep valley in the desert

Zoom bag: flight suit

QUOTE:

"I WISH THE AMERICANS WELL AND PRAY NONE OF THEIR SONS WILL DIE AND THAT ALL THE PEOPLE OF IRAQ ARE GRATEFUL TO NOBLE SOULS IN AMERICA DEMONSTRATING AGAINST THE WAR. . . . LOTS OF BLOOD WILL BE SHED, LOTS OF BLOOD — WE ARE REFERRING TO BLOOD ON EVERY SIDE: AMERICAN, FRENCH, SAUDI BLOOD AND IRAQI." *—PRESIDENT SADDAM HUSSEIN, AS TOLD TO CNN'S PETER ARNETT, JANUARY 28, 1991*

QUOTE:

"HALFWAY AROUND THE WORLD WE ARE ENGAGED IN A GREAT STRUGGLE IN THE SKIES AND ON THE SEAS AND SANDS. WE KNOW WHY WE'RE THERE. WE ARE AMERICANS, PART OF SOMETHING LARGER THAN OURSELVES. FOR TWO CENTURIES, WE'VE DONE THE HARD WORK OF FREEDOM. AND TONIGHT WE LEAD THE WORLD IN FACING DOWN A THREAT TO DECENCY AND HUMANITY." *—PRESIDENT GEORGE BUSH, STATE OF THE UNION ADDRESS, JANUARY 29, 1991*

CHAPTER 4

Green Terror

The War and the Environment

"Torching oil wells and disgorging crude into the gulf, Saddam makes the planet his latest victim."

—Richard Lacayo, "A War Against the Earth," *Time*, February 4, 1991

What did President Bush mean when he said that Saddam Hussein is an environmental terrorist?

War is never gentle or kind, and when two or more countries are at war against one another, there are certain violent acts and practices that are deemed "responsible" within the conventions of war. These include things like dropping bombs and fighting hand to hand, practices that would be considered heinous during peacetime. It is expected that some soldiers from the warring countries will be killed or wounded; there has yet to be a bloodless war. But it is also assumed that countries not at war will be left alone. These include neutral countries that share borders with countries at war.

President Bush called Saddam Hussein an environmental terrorist because Saddam has threatened — and, indeed, has begun — to use the destruction of the environment as a weapon of war. We all need clean air to breathe and clean water to drink, regardless of whether our nations are at war. By hurting the environment, Saddam is hurting combatants and noncombatants alike.

In the case of the intentional oil spills caused by Saddam Hussein in the Persian Gulf, the citizens of all the countries that border on the Gulf — Iran, Iraq, Kuwait, Saudi Arabia, Bahrain, Qatar, and the United Arab Emirates — are suffering the immediate effects of environmental destruction. The Kuwaiti oil pumped into the Gulf has destroyed shrimp and other food sources for the region's six million people, has threatened the area's water supply, and has killed countless numbers of fish and other wildlife. Should Saddam make good on his threat to unleash chemical and biological weapons, the zone of destruction could be much larger — and the effects absolutely horrendous.

In addition to pumping oil into the Gulf, Saddam has threatened to set fire to Kuwait's oil wells. What are the potential long-term consequences of these actions?

The possible long-term consequences of the oil spill are enormous. The slick is a ten-mile-long band of crude oil, as thick as mud on the surface of the water. Hundreds of dead birds already are washing up on the shores of Saudi Arabia, and tar has begun to sink to the bottom of the Gulf — killing coral reefs and other marine life that serve as food for fish.

Experts tell us that the Gulf is the most complex and delicate marine ecosystem in the world, an average of only 110 feet deep. Remember the Exxon *Valdez* oil spill in Prince William Sound in Alaska? The spill in the Persian Gulf has involved twenty-five times the amount of oil leaked into the water by the *Valdez*. And whereas Prince William Sound flushes itself naturally every few weeks, experts say the Persian Gulf flushes itself much more infrequently. Estimates range from as little as three years to as long as a century.

To make matters worse, the cleanup efforts in the Gulf have, of course, been hampered by the war. Oil that is not promptly contained mixes with the water and turns into a thick, muddy substance that is more difficult to combat. If Saddam continues to release oil into the Gulf, the region's ecosystems may be beyond saving.

As if the release of oil into the Gulf weren't bad enough, Saddam has also been accused of having mined many of Kuwait's 363 operating oil wells. If these wells are ignited, ten million barrels of oil could burn each day, producing a 620,000-square-mile cloud of dark, sooty smoke every twenty-four hours. The smoke would foul the air and block sunlight as far east as Afghanistan and northern India. The fires could burn out of control for months, even years. Experts estimate that after thirty days, this oily, black smoke could hang over an area nearly half the size of the United States, decreasing solar energy by 20 percent. This blanket of smoke could lower surface temperatures in the Indian subcontinent anywhere from four to five degrees, bringing frosts in spring and disrupting monsoon rains. Damage to crops and wildlife would be devastating.

"Between the oil spills and the fires, the creation of toxic waste by the military, and the potential use of chemical and even nuclear weapons, this is clearly a conflict with grave environmental consequences," says Owen Byrd, senior adviser at Bay Area Action, a California-based environmental group that grew out of the 1990 Earth Day campaign.

What kinds of wildlife live in the Gulf region, and how are they being affected by the war?

Experts estimate that twenty-seven species are threatened by the oil spill alone. According to Richard Hobson, an information officer at the Royal Embassy of Saudi Arabia in Washington, D.C., the Gulf is of relatively shallow water, similar to the warm waters of the Gulf of Mexico or the Atlantic off the coast of Florida. In those waters are a number of varieties of extremely colorful, semitropical fish, says Hobson, including parrot fish, spotted angelfish, lemon butterfly fish, and lionfish. The Gulf is also home to grouper, a very popular food source in the region. These fish feed on offshore coral reefs, which are endangered by the spill. As a result, the fish that manage to survive the direct effects of the oil-soaked Gulf will be threatened by a significant decrease in their food supply.

Other types of wildlife threatened by the spill include several species of shark, one of which is the whale shark, the largest fish in the ocean; porpoises; dolphins; and sea walruses. (According to Hobson, many people believe that the legend of mermaids grew from ancient mariners' spotting these sea walruses. In Arabic, these walruses are called *arus al-bahr*, which means "Bride of the Sea.") Sea walruses, which are mammals, must come to the surface to breathe, and they have a difficult time doing so when oil covers the water. They are also at risk because they feed on sea grass, also damaged by the oil.

Many of us have seen pictures of dead or suffering cormorants, the bird most commonly associated with the Gulf region. But hundreds and hundreds of other birds, such as gulls and terns, have also been threatened or killed by the spill, says Hobson. Another victim of the spill is the flamingo, the beautiful pink migratory bird that inhabits the Gulf's shallow waters from November until the summer months, when the weather becomes too hot for them.

Environmentalists and others are also concerned about the fate of several varieties of sea turtle — such as the green turtle (most common) and the hawksbill — that make their homes in the Gulf. In a fascinating ritual, the female turtles leave the male and young turtles behind every few years and come ashore — the only time they do so — to nest and lay eggs. In addition to the risk of suffocating in the water, the oil slick could also prevent these turtles from being able to climb up on land to perpetuate their already endangered species.

What does Saddam Hussein hope to gain from environmental terrorism?

Most likely, Saddam hopes that environmental terrorism will give him an advantage not just militarily, but psychologically as well. By threatening to wreak massive destruction on the world's ecosystems, Saddam gains control of a power denied him militarily. He wants his enemies to know that he cannot be attacked with impunity: Anyone who takes him on must be willing to pay an enormous price.

But when Saddam ordered oil to be emptied into the Gulf, he may have been motivated by military considerations as well. Releasing the oil without warning created a great likelihood that tar balls would be formed, quickly choking the Saudi desalination plants. Those plants supply Saudi Arabia and the United Arab Emirates — and the Allied troops — with fresh water. A disruption of the enemy's water supply certainly would produce a military advantage.

There has also been speculation that Saddam unleashed the oil in an attempt to prevent an amphibious liberation of Kuwait. The Pentagon has denied that a slick would prevent such an assault, but as *Newsweek* (February 4, 1991) noted, "The allies would have to factor the oil flood into their battle plans. The vents on amphibious tractors that would carry soldiers onto the beaches would be fouled by oily water. Unless special piping were added to the vents, soldiers would have to assume exposed positions atop the vehicles to manually clear the intake and exhaust valves."

Have there ever been other acts of environmental terrorism during times of peace or war?

"Throughout history, our ecosystem has been victimized by wartime practices," says Bay Area Action's Owen Byrd. "The use of modern weapons and strategies now means that war against anyone is war against the Earth. We are still paying the consequences of Agent Orange [a chemical used during the Vietnam War to defoliate trees], both ecologically and in terms of the health of the people exposed to it."

Environmental destruction as a weapon of war is nothing new. The ancient Romans mixed salt into the fields of their enemies to ensure that their crops would fail for generations. What has changed is the extent to which warriors today can affect the Earth's ecosystem. Our modern technological capabilities allow destruction on a scale never before seen.

> **QUOTE:**
>
> **"HURT NOT THE EARTH, NEITHER THE SEA, NOR THE TREES."** — *THE REVELATION OF ST. JOHN THE DIVINE 7:3*

It's interesting to note that nations have moved much more quickly to agree on protections for individual human lives than for the life of our planet. Forty-eight nations and the Holy See (the Vatican) have signed the Geneva Conventions, four international agreements intended to protect soldiers and civilians from the effects of war. But no international laws make it a crime to harm the environment during war. Saddam Hussein has made it painfully clear that the long-term effects of his assaults on the environment will not serve to deter him. Unless measures are taken to prevent additional harm to the environment, the world may suffer the effects of this war for a long, long time.

What can Americans do to lessen our dependence on oil and to use energy more efficiently?

Ericka Kurz, campaign coordinator of the Students' Environmental Action Coalition (SEAC) in Chapel Hill, North Carolina, stresses the need for young people to work together to put an end to our energy crisis. "Acting individually and changing your habits to be more energy efficient helps," Kurz says, "but young people also have the energy and the awareness to band together and really push for some changes." SEAC is currently lobbying in support of a Department of Energy bill which eventually would require that every car in the United States get a minimum of forty to forty-five miles per gallon of gas. "There are a lot of high school students out there who are forming schoolwide campus energy policies," Kurz says. "Encouraging your school to insulate, to use compact fluorescent lightbulbs, and to provide more school buses or car-pooling services can make a huge difference."

Other things you can do:

- **Recycle**. Making one ton of recycled paper uses only about 60 percent of the energy needed to make a ton of virgin paper. (*The Recycler's Handbook,* Earthworks Press, 1990)
- **Lower your home's temperature by six degrees.** According to the U.S. Department of Energy, if every household did that for only twenty-four hours, we could save more than 570,000 barrels of oil.
- **Plant trees around your home** Shady trees could cut your energy bills and use of electricity by 10 to 50 percent in the summer months, says The American Forestry Association in Washington, D.C..
- **Drive less**. If 1 percent of the car owners in America left their cars idle for one day a week, it would save an estimated forty-two million gallons of gas a year. (*50 Simple Things You Can Do to Save the Earth,* Earthworks Press, 1989)
- **Limit the length of your hot showers; avoid hot baths.** The U.S. Department of Energy has determined that water heaters are the second-largest residential energy user.

"I think that some Iraqi teens feel the same way we do. It's a war between people, not a war with birds and fish. These innocent animals are getting punished for doing absolutely nothing. The environment has nothing to do with the war. The fighting should be between two armed forces. The whole situation is a horror. I think that some teens in Iraq are in complete support of Saddam and see it as a holy war; others see both sides, especially since people in Iraq have been defecting."—*Terry, an eleventh grader from Springfield, Vermont*

"It makes no sense what Saddam is doing. He's not too swift. It especially makes no sense what he's doing to the environment. These acts are not helping him, and they're only hurting the world. The Iraqi teens are probably not that well informed, and there is no way they can understand what's going on there."—*Matt, an eighth grader from New York, New York*

"What Saddam did to the environment was a totally uncalled-for tactic and a terrorist act. It did nothing to hurt the U.S. or any other country physically. The only thing that got damaged was the environment. All the nature and the animals are the ones who are suffering. I think that Iraqi teens are probably behind Saddam in these acts because they don't know any better. They've all been brainwashed."—*Kris, an eleventh grader from Columbia, Tennessee*

"Saddam's acts against the environment are purely terrorist acts. There is no sense to his having harmed the fish or the environment. Teens in Iraq are probably as confused as I am about what's going on, but I believe that they probably support him, because that's how they've been trained."—*Beth, a twelfth grader from Norcross, Georgia*

"The teens probably think that there was a reason that Saddam did what he did to the environment. For all they know, Saddam's acts are to protect his country. They are being taught this, and Saddam is their ruler and they stand behind him. The environment didn't do anything to Iraq, but still the animals — and nature — got killed off."—*David, a twelfth grader from Alvarado, Texas*

"I think Iraqi teenagers don't know what's happening. What they see in their newspapers is what Saddam and his officials put in the paper. All they know is that the United States is bombing Iraq and we are the bad guys. Probably the only idea about the oil spill that they've heard is that we hit an oil tanker or a refinery. They assume that the U.S. was the sole reason for the spill. Actually, I think that teenagers in Iraq, and the general public there, don't know any better. They know what their newspapers tell them."—*Tony, a twelfth grader from Paramus, New Jersey*

"I think Iraqi teens probably are disgusted with Saddam's actions on the environment and what he has done. Saddam is ruining the world by breaking everything apart, and, most important, he's ruining the environment. The environment has not done anything to him, but, then again, he is a crazy man. Some of the teens may not know what to believe, because, after all, he is their ruler and they stand behind him. I would hope, though, that they would be against him for what he has done to the environment."—*Sarah, a tenth grader from New Orleans, Louisiana*

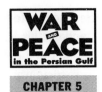
Spectator War

The War and the Media

"In a time when close-up pictures from the front are no farther away than a TV producer's fingertip, the ability of war to intrude upon our daily lives is unlimited. In the scheme of things, it is terrible to be bombed, strafed, rocketed, shelled, missiled, or otherwise fricasseed by high explosives.

"It is almost as bad to have loved ones on either end of the bombing, strafing, and so forth. And for many millions of Americans heartsick at the deceptively antiseptic high-tech air war against Iraq, the incessant barrage of war news is a bombardment of intense psychological impact. The Bad News Syndrome. Or as one shrink labels it, 'the CNN Complex.'"
—David Nyhan, "Welcome to the Persian Gulf Bowl,"
the *Boston Globe,* January 27, 1991

How accurate have radio and television coverage of events in the Persian Gulf been?

The war in the Persian Gulf is an ideal made-for-television action adventure, complete with high stakes, heroism, intrigue — and a villain straight from Central Casting. But the very technology that allows television to bring us the war news almost instantaneously also increases the risk that all of the reports we hear will not have been confirmed.

An alarming example of an inaccurate report making its way to us via satellite took place early in the war. "It's gas, it's gas," screamed a reporter live from Israel when the first Iraqi Scuds hit that country. We soon discovered that only conventional warheads had been used, but the fear had already been instilled.

Overall, however, the American public gives good grades to the media for its coverage of the war. A Times Mirror poll released on January 31, 1991, reported that 72 percent of respondents believed "news organizations are attempting to deliver to the public an objective picture of the conflict."

Piers Wood, chief of staff of the Center for Defense Information in Washington, D.C., says that "print coverage of the war has been excellent" but that "initial television reports have been highly inaccurate. They could have waited until they had all the facts instead of blurting out what they thought they were hearing and seeing before they really knew."

Television news producers have been faced with difficult choices during this conflict. Americans have come to count on war coverage that's comprehensive and immediate. We expect live coverage, yet we also demand the level of journalistic accuracy and professionalism found in carefully prepared and edited reports. We may not be able to have both.

"Everyone is hungry for information, and when kids have free periods they come into the library and watch CNN. All the books about the Middle East are on display, and students look at them. We get the *New York Times* and the *Christian Science Monitor,* as well as the *Toledo Blade,* and students are reading newspapers. Students are doing papers in history on each of the countries in the Middle East, and they're doing time lines on the recent events in that part of the world. Some kids are upset by the news. It seems too close. They can't step away from it. Others find it thrilling." —*Vicki Koelsch, librarian, Maumee Valley Country Day School, Toledo, Ohio*

What has been the level of censorship on news in the United States during the war in the Gulf?

The outcomes of wars in the twentieth century are dependent almost as much on information — and disinformation — as they are on bullets and high-tech equipment. Knowledge of troop movements, enemy morale, and the precision with which targets have been hit all play a role in the strategy of warfare. That's why the U.S. government and the military clamp restrictions on an otherwise free press in times of war.

Despite the extensive media coverage of the war, the American public really doesn't know all that much about the events unfolding in the Persian Gulf. Information coming out of the Pentagon is sketchy at best, and reports from overseas are carefully screened by military censors. Some members of the media have complained that their access to

> **QUOTE:**
>
> "THERE IS A BEAST OF A WAR OUT THERE, AN ELEPHANT WE'RE TRYING TO DESCRIBE. BASED ON THE INFORMATION WE'RE GIVEN, WE'RE ABOUT AT THE TOENAIL RANGE." —*FORREST SAWYER ON ABC-TV'S "NIGHTLINE"*

information has been restricted beyond the bounds of reasonableness. They point out, for example, that members of the press have been denied access to B-52 bomber pilots, presumably because the bombs dropped from the B-52s have resulted in heavy civilian casualties.

By and large, however, the American public has indicated its willingness to accept restrictions placed on the press during this conflict. In fact, the Times Mirror poll previously mentioned found that 57 percent of respondents believe that "the military should increase its control over reporting of the war." Americans are willing to forgo information for the sake of national security, even when that information would not seem to affect the safety of the troops.

The Center for Defense Information's Piers Wood disagrees with reports that the military has purposely misled the press and given out information known to be inaccurate. "The military leaders have been great — direct and forthright," he says. "Yet I think that the American military has been telling the truth. Still there may be a need later on to use the press as part of the deception of Saddam Hussein, and I hope that the military trusts our journalists enough to do so. In World War II, the military always trusted the press, and I hope that we've returned to that. Maybe some great ruse will be perpetrated on Saddam Hussein — and we might need the help of the press to tell him the big lie."

What is the official "press pool"? How are members chosen?

A "pool" is a select group of journalists who are permitted by the U.S. military to cover the war firsthand. At present, eleven press pools are covering the war in the Gulf; most of these consist of six or seven video, print, and radio journalists. Major news organizations possess permanent slots in the pools and rotate reporters in and out. The remaining slots are filled by representatives of other media organizations. In order to be accepted into a pool, each member of the press must pass a physical exam. And, as a condition of receiving credentials, journalists must sign a consent form indicating that they will adhere to military ground rules. They must agree not to reveal those ground rules because identifying the limits of what can be reported might be helpful to the Iraqis and to potential terrorists.

Pool correspondents cover the war for all of the news agencies. Any information they get must be shared. Thus far, that information has been relatively minimal. Press coverage of the war in the Gulf has been restricted to a much greater extent than in the past. During the Vietnam conflict, for example, members of the press were allowed free access to any area of the country under U.S. control. In the Persian Gulf, press pools are under the close supervision of a military guide at all times. Military escorts monitor all interviews with the troops. And all press reports are subject to censorship.

> **QUESTION FOR DISCUSSION:**
>
> WHERE SHOULD ONE DRAW THE LINE BETWEEN THE NEED FOR CENSORSHIP AND THE PROTECTION OF FREEDOM OF THE PRESS IN TIMES OF WAR?

Many members of the press are concerned that the flow of war news to the United States is being too narrowly channeled by the numerous restrictions placed on the press pools. They complain that military censors are working not just to prevent the leakage of sensitive information but also to protect the image of the military. At the same time, however, journalists concede that the majority of their stories are being returned without significant deletions.

"I'm really unsettled about this war. It bothers me because I'm not clear how strongly I feel. I'm behind the U.S., but I'm not sure what the right answers are because I think sometimes that the news is distorted. I want to know the facts." —*Kevin, a twelfth grader from Gainesville, Florida*

What is the role of propaganda in war?

Propaganda is any information or idea meant to win support for, or create opposition to, a government or a cause. The information may be true or false, but it is always selected for its political effect.

Propaganda can have a phenomenal impact on an entire people and has shaped the course of history. Hitler's Nazi Ministry of Propaganda, headed by Paul Joseph Goebbels, was one of the most effective users of the art of propaganda. Goebbels made skillful use of the mass media to promote the cause of Nazism throughout Germany. The Allies responded in kind, distributing posters, for example, that depicted the enemy as subhuman creatures in an effort to further inflame feelings against them.

> **QUOTE:**
>
> "THE FIRST CASUALTY WHEN WAR COMES IS TRUTH." — *SENATOR HIRAM JOHNSON* (1917)

Propaganda has been an important tool in the war in the Persian Gulf as well. Saddam Hussein's claim that the Allied forces had intentionally bombed a baby formula factory apparently was intended to raise the ire of Arabs as well as convince citizens of the Allied nations that their troops were engaged in acts of brutality. The Pentagon insists that the factory bombed was really used to make biological weapons.

Oftentimes, Saddam's use of propaganda has backfired. His parading around of Allied POWs served not to lessen the will of the Allies, as he had believed, but actually to strengthen their conviction that Saddam must be stopped. Saddam also failed to achieve his intended effect early in the crisis when he held televised meetings with the Americans and Europeans held hostage in Iraq. What he considered proof of his "hospitality" was seen by Westerners as a frightening charade.

The Allies remain optimistic about their troops' insusceptibility to Iraqi propaganda. Ann Crawford, publisher and editor of *Military Living*, a magazine for members of the military and their families, says, "Propaganda may be a traditional presence during any wartime, but I don't think our soldiers in the Middle East are affected by it. Even if they listen to it or are unwillingly exposed to it, my feeling is that they find it amusing. It's more comical than anything else."

Who is Baghdad Betty?

One of the images transmitted most frequently to the American public over the months of Operation Desert Shield was that of American soldiers stationed in the Saudi Arabian desert — listening to the radio. Those of you who remember the story of Adrian Cronauer, the popular American disk jockey portrayed by Robin Williams in *Good Morning, Vietnam,* are probably aware that radio is and has traditionally been a soldier's best friend — a source of information and entertainment.

"During wars, there are usually radio shows that originate in each warring nation and are specifically designed to antagonize and provoke the soldiers of the enemy country," says an editor on the *Washington Post*'s foreign news desk. "Baghdad Betty is said to be a woman disk jockey on Iraqi radio. But she is much more than a disk jockey — she is a propagandist. She teases the Allied soldiers and tries to shake their morale by saying things like, 'GI, you should be home. While you're gone, Robert Redford is kissing your girlfriend. Tom Selleck is dating your lady.'" Baghdad Betty is often compared to "Tokyo Rose," a disk jockey who transmitted from Japan during World War II. But reports indicate that Baghdad Betty is far from accomplishing her goals. Her ignorance of American culture is said to have left GIs howling with laughter and deliberately tuning in to her show just for a good dose of entertainment. Her best-known flub thus far has been the statement in which she warned that while Americans were sweltering in the Saudi sun, their wives and girlfriends were home making love to . . . cartoon character Bart Simpson.

TEENSPEAK:

Do you think the Pentagon has put too much restriction on the news coming out of the Persian Gulf?

"Yes. The public gets the news, but we don't get the actual details of casualties. It really is not fair, because people should know what is going on, and the Pentagon is hiding news from us." —*Jane, a twelfth grader from Greenwich, Connecticut*

"I don't think the Pentagon has put too much restriction on the news. I think if we see too much, then there could be problems with security and planning with the troops. It would be really bad in terms of the troops. I think the Pentagon keeps the public well informed, and there is no reason we should have every detail." —*Daniel, a twelfth grader from Marietta, Georgia*

"I think the Pentagon is correct in the way they are revealing the news. If too much news comes out of the Persian Gulf, it will turn out to be like Vietnam. With more restriction, it will help our troops fight a better war. Also, too much negative news will affect the public's view about the war." —*Jason, a twelfth grader from Warwick, Rhode Island*

"The Pentagon has not left out too much information. We can't let everything be announced over the television. We have to control the news because the media is worldwide and we have to protect the safety of our troops. If we disclose too much information, then Saddam will make plans on different ways to attack our troops. It's really important to keep the information coming out of the Pentagon low-key. It is very easy for Iraqis to pick up information off of CNN. I really think we are pretty well informed by the media of generally what's going on, but they have to limit the details." —*Stephen, an eleventh grader from Louisville, Kentucky*

"I think the Pentagon has put too much restriction on the news coming out of the Gulf. I feel particularly bad for the people who have friends and family over there and have no idea what is going on as far as casualties are concerned. I understand that the Pentagon has to be careful in what they say over the news, but they could at least keep us up to date as far as casualties are concerned. I am not saying that the Pentagon should reveal any military strategies and plans, but they could keep the public more informed."—*Sarah, a twelfth grader from Falls Church, Virginia*

"The Pentagon is doing a great job on restricting what comes out of the Persian Gulf. I think it is really important because Saddam could pick up military strategies from CNN if the news is revealed. CNN has to be careful on how much is being said over the wire so that Saddam can't attack our troops." —*Jeff, a tenth grader from Phoenix, Arizona*

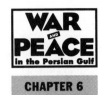
Hitting Home

How the War Affects Americans

"If I could ask Saddam Hussein one question, it would be what prompted him to invade Kuwait and start all this fighting. He has ruined a lot of people's lives. I truly wish he never had."
—Amanda Abraham, an eighth grader from Garden City, New York

"My Father's Been Activated": Amanda Abraham's Story

The week we started this book, we heard from our friend Amanda Abraham, an eighth grader at Garden City Middle School in Garden City, New York. Amanda is one of the co-authors of *Greetings from High School*, another book in the "Peterson's H.S." series. She was very sad. Her father, a doctor, is in the Army reserves and has been activated, probably for a year or more. For now, he's training at Walter Reed Army Hospital in Washington, D.C., but he could be sent to the Persian Gulf at any time. We interviewed Amanda the first evening her father was gone.

"I hadn't been following the war very much, but I'm against war. Somehow I never expected that my father would end up in it. This hasn't happened to anyone else I know, and I don't think that I want to get involved with support groups or anything because I hate the entire idea of war and don't want to be doing things that remind me about how awful what's going on is. I guess that I'll have to count more on my mother — and she on me — but. . . .

"Still, I think that we had to do what we had to do. War seemed to be the only thing we could do to stop Saddam. I have nothing against kids from Iraq, or even Iraqi civilians, however. I think that teenagers and everyone in Iraq have to be scared . . . the way I am. My younger brother, who is eight, is scared, too, but I'm not sure how much he really understands."

What is the purpose of all the support groups across America? Must one have a loved one stationed overseas to join a support group?

Families of soldiers in the Gulf need to know there are people to whom they can turn when they're feeling down and worried. Marine Staff Sergeant Ronald McCants, a reservist who has been stationed at Quantico, in Virginia, since January 25, 1991, staffs a support hotline. He takes calls from people who wish to speak with a counselor and provides referrals. "A friendly word or two" makes all the difference to those who are suffering because a family member or members have been deployed, McCants says. He adds, "It's easy for me to relate to what family members feel since my wife and three children are really upset and scared by the prospect that on any given day I might be sent to Saudi Arabia."

Anyone who feels that he or she would benefit from a support group is eligible to attend meetings or to get involved, says McCants, regardless of whether he or she has an association with a soldier.

FACT:

AMERICAN WOMEN SEEM TO BE MORE STRESSED OUT BY THE WAR THAN ARE AMERICAN MEN. "THE PEOPLE, THE PRESS, AND THE WAR IN THE GULF," A POLL RELEASED AS A SPECIAL TIMES MIRROR NEWS INTEREST INDEX ON JANUARY 31, 1991, FOUND THAT:

•41 PERCENT OF THE WOMEN SURVEYED SAID THAT THEY FEEL UNHAPPY, AS COMPARED WITH 23 PERCENT OF THE MEN;

•64 PERCENT OF THE WOMEN REPORTED FEELING DEPRESSED ABOUT THE WAR, AS COMPARED WITH 33 PERCENT OF THE MEN; AND

•21 PERCENT OF THE WOMEN REPORTED THAT THEY HAVE A TOUGH TIME CONCENTRATING BECAUSE THEY'RE WORRIED ABOUT THE WAR, AS COMPARED WITH 8 PERCENT OF THE MEN.

TEENSPEAK:

Two Points of View

"I'm going to tell you that I am a Palestinian, an American Palestinian, and I think that the Americans should have minded their own business. I think that it is absolutely wrong of the U.S. to have gone into Iraq. The only reason the Americans are there is economics. The U.S. and Britain always do things like this. It's massive murder — they're killing innocent people. The news in the U.S. is so distorted — I see news footage that proves that civilians are being killed.

"It's disgusting that there has been no uproar about the Israeli bombings killing innocent Palestinian citizens . . . Iraqi teens have grown up knowing war. What kinds of feelings do you think people there have? They're almost numb, and they're angry. They hate Americans.

"Kids my age in Iraq have lived through war after war. The real distressing thing is that again it's Arabs fighting Arabs, besides the Americans, who are there wrongfully. My grandfather lives in Saudi Arabia, and he's frightened to death about this war. But I believe that he will survive. I feel it in my heart."
—*Haneen, a twelfth grader from Bethesda, Maryland*

"My father is Israeli, and my grandparents live in Tel Aviv — they have lived in Israel since the time that the country was formed. Never before did they consider coming to the United States to live. But after the recent events, they have come to live with my family in New Jersey.

"Israel is used to war. My grandparents have lived through five of them. When Iraq invaded Kuwait in August, my grandparents were visiting us here in the U.S., and my mother was very concerned. She wanted them to consider staying here. But my grandfather has been very tough — even after the bombings, he considered leaving because if he didn't he would be weakening to Saddam Hussein's scare tactics. But my grandparents are in their seventies, and they went through night after night of no sleep, of having to get up and put on their gas masks. It just wasn't a nice way to live.

"I was watching my grandparents as they listened to President Bush's State of the Union address shortly after they arrived in the States. They are so supportive of America and really feel threatened about the fact that some people here are not behind the war. They know all too well that if it hadn't been for America's Patriot missiles, Israel would be in terrible shape right now."—*Ron, a twelfth grader from Tenafly, New Jersey*

How can one check on the status of family members in the Gulf?

The Pentagon has set up toll-free numbers to be used by relatives of service members stationed in the Gulf:

Air Force:	(800) 253-9276
Army:	(800) 626-1440 (immediate family only)
Coast Guard:	(800) 367-8724
Marines:	(800) 523-2694 (immediate family only)
Navy:	(800) 255-3808 (immediate family only)
	(800) 732-1206 (other relatives and friends)

Callers will be asked for the exact spelling of the serviceperson's last name and, when possible, should provide rank, Social Security number, and military unit.

The Joint Chiefs of Staff have ordered the American Red Cross to discontinue transmitting messages to members of the military except in "life and death" emergencies. Messages concerning birth, death, serious illness, and serious child-care disruptions involving immediate family members can still be transmitted by the International Committee of the Red Cross.

If you would like to send a letter of support to the troops, write to:

Any Service Member
Land-based Personnel
Operation Desert Storm
APO
New York, NY 09848-0006

or

Any Service Member
Ship-based Personnel
Operation Desert Storm
FPO
New York, NY 09866-0006

Soldiers love receiving mail. Meyera Oberndorf, mayor of Virginia Beach, Virginia, has already received hundreds — if not thousands — of letters from soldiers who want to thank her and the good people of Virginia Beach for their gifts, which have included six tons of M&Ms and Turkish Taffy, as well as 20,000 paperback books. Mayor Oberndorf shared with us one thank-you note that she received from two "Desert Rats" (members of the Royal Scottish Army). They wrote, "Serving alongside the U.S. Marine Corps in our 120-mm battle tanks. . . . We are very keen to make new pen friends from across the Atlantic. We would like to hear more about your wonderful city as we have never been to the U.S.A."

"I've Enlisted": James Casper's Story

James Casper is a senior at Clearfield High School in Clearfield, Utah. This past September he joined the Navy. He will begin serving for a minimum of two years once he graduates from high school.

"I support what we're doing in the Middle East, and I hope that the war ends early because I worry that we are risking people's lives. I hope that Saddam realizes what he's up against.

"The thing that I wonder about is what ever gave Saddam Hussein the idea that he could beat the United States. Sometimes I think about the people of Iraq — they have such a different outlook on life. The Muslim religion teaches you that if you die in combat, you go to heaven. Religious feeling is so strong there that some teenagers probably look forward to going to heaven because that's what is taught to them from the time that they're small children.

"I'm sure that the teenagers in Iraq are scared because their lives are threatened. I feel that I will do America right by going over there and fighting for my country. I'm proud to go.

"The one thing that annoys me are the people who are antiwar, who I believe are violating the rights of our country. I think that they should be thrown in jail, but, then again, everyone has the right to their own opinions."

SPOTLIGHT:
Main Street, U.S.A.

Mayor Homer "Buddy" DeLoach talks about how the war in the Gulf has affected the town of Hinesville, Georgia:

"Kids have to realize that what the soldiers are doing is so important for the entire world. When our freedom is threatened, we have to have people who are willing to go and serve. In a community like ours, where military folks make up about 50 percent of the population, people have to band together. Church groups have formed; neighborhood groups have formed. On some streets, almost all the men are gone. Communitywide prayer services have been scheduled.

"For teenagers in our town, well, teenagers react differently. Some are more frightened than others. They spend a lot of time together; they rely on one another. There's a real emphasis on their not being glued to the television. For a big part of their days, they have to go on being teenagers, just like teenagers everywhere. There is so much hanging over them, when a parent is gone. Support groups have been organized by the schools. Counselors and psychologists have set up programs in the schools. What they are doing is mentioning the situation every day and encouraging teens to talk about how they're feeling. Some kids talk freely and others don't.

"That George Bush came to town is just wonderful for all of us — the attention makes all of us realize the importance of our contribution to America, to the world."

How are American children being affected emotionally and psychologically by the war in the Persian Gulf?
Dr. James Garbarino, president of the Chicago-based Erikson Institute for

Advanced Studies in Child Development, has spent several years studying young people who have grown up in war zones. He has found that war can have a wide range of effects on youngsters, regardless of whether it's being fought on their homefront or not. "Many young people here in the United States are experiencing anxiety, different from fear in that it is free-floating and not linked to a specific cause," says Dr. Garbarino. A number of eight-year-olds whom Dr. Garbarino has interviewed in recent weeks have expressed sadness — sadness caused by the harsh reality of death and killing.

Despite being thousands of miles away, the war in the Persian Gulf has become a very personal war for American children. "A number of young-sters, when asked whether they know an American soldier stationed in the Middle East, reply that they do," says Dr. Garbarino. "Upon further investigation, it becomes apparent that in many cases the person whom they claim to know is someone they have never met or come into contact with — such as a teacher's brother or a friend's father. This indicates that young people are experiencing a very broad sense of connection with the war — it is hitting home on an inward level, even those young people who are not at risk of losing a parent or other family member."

> **QUOTE:**
>
> "A SIMPLE CHILD, THAT LIGHTLY DRAWS ITS BREATH, AND FEELS ITS LIFE IN EVERY LIMB, WHAT SHOULD IT KNOW OF DEATH?"— *WILLIAM WORDSWORTH*

Many children also fear for their own safety. They worry that Iraq will drop a bomb on the United States, and they are concerned that they haven't been given the gas masks that they see Israeli children using. It's difficult for young children to separate themselves from what they see on television news and hear their parents and other adults discussing. The concept of physical distance can be particularly confusing. For example, many younger children have difficulty understanding why they can't hear the bombs dropping on Baghdad and Tel Aviv.

The responsibility for allaying kids' fears has fallen not only on the shoulders of parents, but on schools, as well. Experts estimate that not since the explosion of the space shuttle *Challenger* in 1986 have American schools had to deal with such a large number of depressed, frightened, and upset young people. Child psychologists recommend that parents and teachers take the time to talk to children about their fears and answer any questions they may have. It's particularly important to help kids understand that they are safe. Older children should be able to grasp the fact that Iraq is more than 7,000 miles away from the United States, but they may need maps and detailed explanations to be convinced.

Are American school kids vulnerable to terrorist attacks?

It's no secret that Saddam Hussein has called upon the followers of Islam around the world to perpetrate acts of terrorism against the nations of the Allied coalition. And, to a certain degree, Americans have reacted to those threats. Airlines report a sharp drop in American travel overseas, and security precautions have been taken to protect buildings and facilities considered likely targets. But experts on terrorism insist that the United States is relatively safe from terrorist attack. They say Americans are much more likely to be struck and killed by a car while crossing a busy city street than they are to be killed by a terrorist act.

On an ABC news special on January 26, 1991, Admiral William Crowe, former chairman of the Joint Chiefs of Staff (the position that Colin Powell now holds), commented on the threat of terrorism in the United States: "Certainly Saddam Hussein would like to conduct terrorism against the United States. He's made that crystal clear. I don't think in military terms it would be very significant, and I think he would have real difficulty reaching the United States. But he might be able to mount a single or a few terrorist acts that would be very unfortunate. . . . But you must not let terrorism or the threat of terrorism dictate what you do. That just encourages terrorists and makes it worse. You must decide what is right and wrong and then do it and continue to do it. And what children can do in their everyday lives is continue to live as they usually do, and do it without fear."

SPOTLIGHT:

Citizen-to-Citizen Ambassadors

As the globe continues to shrink and countries become increasingly interdependent, young people especially have begun to place great value on cultural exchange. Concerned that the war in the Gulf might hamper the efforts of

our youthful ambassadors, we spoke with Scott Ramey, manager of public affairs and spokesperson for the American Field Service.

Do you think that international travel, particularly study-abroad programs, will be affected by the war in the Gulf?

We are concerned about participation in our summer programs, although we do not believe that the work of intercultural exchange or understanding should be affected by the war. At the same time, we do understand that young people are concerned about traveling to regions believed to be potential targets of terrorism. The only country in the Gulf region in which we have an exchange program is Turkey; until recent years, we had programs in Jordan, Iran, and Israel. To accommodate students who still want to travel, we have expanded our programs in Latin America, Asia, Australia, and New Zealand. We strongly encourage students to travel.

Will the war exacerbate the lack of cultural understanding — or negative cultural stereotypes — that your programs try to eliminate?

Many of our Arab students currently studying in the United States have let us know that they do not feel uncomfortable with the current situation. The towns all across the nation in which these Arab students are residing have opened their hearts to these students — even those students whose families at home may be working in a military capacity for their own nations. Our programs attempt to achieve a world that is more just, one whose citizens understand diversity and differences. We see the work that we do as changing the world, one person at a time.

"My Heart Goes Out to the Palestinians": May's Story

May is an American Field Service exchange student who is living with a family in southern California. Her hometown is Giza, Egypt. She plans to go to college in either Egypt or France.

"I came to the United States in September, right after Saddam Hussein took Kuwait. Even though I am enjoying my year in America, I would prefer to be at home, because Egypt is my country. I would like to be with my family now, and I would like to be there to support my president. You ask whether my family is worried about me, but I am the one who should be worried about them, especially my younger brother who attends the American School.

"I know that Saddam is a very smart person, and I was surprised when he took Kuwait, because it is a friendly country. I think that the U.S. took too quick an action when they attacked Iraq. It showed me that they do not understand Arabs. If we are challenged, we have to prove that we are up to the challenge. Saddam Hussein must prove that he is a man — he has to, that is our way.

"I enjoy my school in California, but I miss my friends, especially having the closeness of having a best friend who shares my values. People here are very cool and I enjoy them, but I feel a distance because our points of view are so different. I am against Saddam because he invaded Kuwait, and it does annoy me that he went and invaded an Arab country.

"The Americans are now fighting in the Middle East for the gas, for the oil. If they were there to liberate a country from an aggressor, they would have done the same thing for Palestine, and they didn't. They haven't. The Americans are also probably there because they're fearful that Saddam will get chemical and nuclear weapons. It is my belief that this world will never get ahead until we take these weapons from everyone. That includes Saddam and it includes the United States and it especially includes Israel.

"In America my belief that the Israeli government is crazy is not a popular one. Yet in Israel, the soldiers kill men because children throw stones. That's all the Palestinians have for weapons — rocks.

"Last semester I studied civics. The people in my class believed, as most Americans do, that because I am a Muslim, because I'm an Arab, I hate Jews. This is not true. I hate the Israeli government. I believe in the Jewish religion. What my people don't like is the Israeli government. Even if they were Muslims, we would hate them for treating other people the way they do.

"In Egypt, we have Jewish Egyptians and we get along with them well even though my friends and I support the Palestinians. All we ask is that a small part of Israel should be made Palestine and should be ruled by Palestinians.

"It's crazy that this war had to happen now, when the world was making so much progress. We were so happy for Germany to reunite. The Earth is going to blow up soon from all the bombs. That makes me angry and sad.

"As Arabs, we don't hate Americans. You'd like to think we do. We are human beings, are smart people. We are trying to communicate for peace. Read some history and know what's happening. Americans can be so uninformed. I have been asked if I live in a pyramid. I live in a nice neighborhood in Giza, in a tenth-floor apartment. My aunt's family has the ninth floor. We live fine in Egypt. Yet people here assume I have a camel for transportation, that I live in a pyramid.

"All Americans blindly sympathize with Israel. No one gave any care to what happened to Palestine. The Palestinians have been treated so badly. Yet they still have faith and they plan to go back. They want to go back. I hope that someday they can. And I hope that what's happened in Iraq makes people realize how unfortunate the plight of the Palestinians is."

What can one do to help the POWs?

"There is nothing that Americans can do for POWs except make donations on their behalf," says Skip Baird, spokesperson for the American Red Cross. "Only if you've worked in the chapters, and are familiar with the procedures and the works of the Red Cross, are you eligible to be trained to go on an international assignment. The one other thing that you can do is give blood, but that is not of prime importance since there is no shortage of blood in reserve."

The International Committee of the Red Cross (ICRC) is the official link between prisoners of war and their immediate families. "Once the Red Cross knows of a POW officially," says Baird, "a one-page form, a message form, can be filled out by prisoners of war and get posted through the ICRC. It's impossible right now to communicate with anyone except immediate family members. One other thing: Don't send letters to POWs in Iraq, because it's difficult to tell how a foreign government hostile to us will use what you've sent against American POWs, especially against the person to whom the letter is directed.

"The thing that needs to be emphasized most is that everyone should seek ways in which they can assist local community members whose families have been touched by the war. These families feel helpless, so trying to share their burden is an important thing. Even consider starting a youth group in your own community to help other kids talk about how they're feeling. This sort of thing may not be as glitzy as writing letters to POWs or petitioning foreign governments, but it certainly has a high level of impact on other people's lives."

TEENSPEAK:

How do you cope with fears and pressures related to the United States' being at war?

"The war doesn't really bother me. I have gotten used to it and I try not to think about it. I have three cousins and a very close friend over in the Gulf, and I guess the best thing to do is to keep busy and think positively about everything. In the area where I live, lots of people have family over there. I watch the news so that I can keep up with what's going on. My cousins are in the Air Force, which is pretty stationary, so they are not that scared." —*Kim, a twelfth grader from Valley Springs, Arkansas*

"I try to realize that this war is important from an economic and moral stand-point considering Kuwait needs help. It frightens me that I would have to go if there was a draft. I cope by keeping myself updated by watching CNN. This really helps. We are trying, in our National Honor Society, to make people aware of the war by setting up meetings with Vietnam vets. This way we can make everyone in the school more knowledgeable — and help them through this situation." —*Jeremy, a twelfth grader from Eau Claire, Wisconsin*

"I think that most people in our school are preoccupied with school, and many people don't have family or friends over there. It hasn't hit home, but as we get older it will hit home, I'm sure. Next year I'll be a senior and if the war continues, I'll have friends who could be drafted. I guess the best thing to do is stay informed. There is a political awareness club at my school. This has been going on all year long but now they talk about Persian Gulf issues. And the guidance counselors sent a brochure around to see if anyone had family over there and needed some help." —*Erica, an eleventh grader from Aurora, Colorado*

"Most students at my school don't really think about the war. They watch CNN to keep informed, but it hasn't hit home since the war is taking place a million miles away. It would be different if it was taking place in the United States" —*Greg, a twelfth grader from Bloomfield, Michigan*

"I basically cope with the war by watching CNN and keeping myself informed about what is going on in Iraq. I'm now eighteen years old and would be eligible for the draft. I'm worried about that, but hopefully it won't come to that." —*Jody, a twelfth grader from Fayetteville, West Virginia*

"In most of my classes in school we talk about the war, which is a real help. My friends have the same fears I do and we talk them over. A lot of teenagers are scared that they're going to get drafted. I keep myself informed by watching NBC and flipping through the different channels because we don't get CNN." —*Tanya, a twelfth grader from Morgantown, West Virginia*

"I cope with the war by talking to my family. My cousin is over there fighting, but we all support him because it was his choice to join the service in the first place. I am not particularly scared. At my school we have counselors who meet with students who have loved ones over there." —*Phil, a tenth grader from Troutdale, Oregon*

"To cope with the war, I talk with my friends and my family. We realize it's not a happy thought about the war and that there will be a lot of casualties, but it had to be done to preserve our country. We had to control Saddam from killing innocent people. I have two cousins over there and most of my friends have close family members there, so we talk it out with one another. It also helps that we talk about the war in all of my classes." —*Warren, a twelfth grader from Montgomery, Alabama*

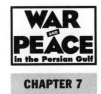

CHAPTER 7

Will Uncle Sam Want You?

Serving in the Military

"I think the draft should be reinstituted if it is necessary. If the war extends too long the draft will definitely be crucial because of all the casualties being suffered. Hopefully, the draft will not have to happen in the first place but if it does, I'm all for it."

—Jim, an eleventh grader in Atlanta, Georgia

How likely is it that there will be a draft?

A draft is highly unlikely. "No, I will not reinstate the draft," President Bush said during a news conference on February 5, 1991, when asked if he could guarantee that military conscription would not be resumed. Reinstatement of the draft would call for an act of Congress, and everyone we contacted within the government assured us that, for the time being, there will be no such act. William Caldwell, a Pentagon spokesperson, told the *New York Times* (February 4, 1991), "The Department of Defense continues to be satisfied that the size of the force we have now, active duty and reservists, is sufficient to do the job. We do not plan to call for a draft. We don't need more people."

The United States has instituted the draft recurrently throughout its history, dating back to the Civil War. The most recent draft was discontinued in 1973, near the end of the Vietnam War, when the military shifted to an all-volunteer force. The draft during the war in Vietnam faced massive opposition in the United States. Congress had made no formal declaration of war, and also a significant number of United States citizens raised moral objections to our country's involvement in Vietnam. As a result, many young men evaded the draft by fleeing to countries, such as Canada and Sweden, that had no agreement with the United States to return "draft dodgers." Today the military relies on incentives such as money for education and job training, as well as a desire to serve one's country, to maintain its forces. (Some critics of the all-volunteer army argue that America thus has a poverty draft: Those who have no other way out of the inner cities sign up for military service so that they can get job skills, an education, or even just a regular paycheck.)

If there were a draft, who would be eligible? Is anyone automatically exempt?

Since the outbreak of war against Iraq, concern over the possibility of a draft has been heard on college campuses and in the halls of high schools. Dr. James Hoyle, a noted pediatrician from the Kelsey Seybold Clinic in Houston, Texas, says, "I have spoken with a number of high school and college students who have expressed fears of the draft. One young man came to speak with me because he strongly believes that he is a conscientious objector. I have also spoken with college students who believe, erroneously, that they will not be drafted, by virtue of the fact that they are in college."

According to a spokesperson at the Selective Service System's national headquarters, if a draft *were* to be reinstated, those called first would be men who turn twenty in the calendar year in which the draft begins. Federal law already requires that all male citizens of the United States register their names and addresses with the Selective Service within thirty days of their eighteenth birthday. The computers of the Selective Service already contain the names and addresses of fourteen million men between the ages of eighteen and twenty-six. The United States Supreme Court ruled in 1981 that Congress could constitutionally exclude women from the draft.

In terms of deferments and postponements, those young men still in high school would be allowed to graduate or turn twenty, whichever came first. College students would either receive postponements until the end of the current semester or, if they were seniors, be given time to graduate.

During the Korean and Vietnam wars, Selective Service regulations provided deferment for college and graduate students. Those student deferments were abolished in 1971.

What are the reserves? What are the duties of members of the reserves?

The reserves are made up of men and women who may hold regular civilian jobs or be full-time students but who are "on call" for the military in times of need. Many people join the reserves in order to obtain financial assistance for their educations. Others join because they feel a sense of duty to their country but are unwilling or unable to commit to the military full-time. Still others join to supplement their incomes.

Reservists must serve on active duty (training) for six months at the beginning of their tenure and then are required to participate in drills one weekend per month and in active duty two weeks out of every year until their service obligation is up. A typical service obligation for a reservist is five and a half years of drill participation and two subsequent years without drill.

In all, the United States has about 1.6 million troops in the reserves and the National Guard. President Bush has authorized the activation of up to a million reservists and Guardsmen for the war in the Persian Gulf.

How much do military personnel make?

Don Betterton, author of *How the Military Will Help You Pay for College* (Peterson's Guides, 1990), says that, as of January 1, 1989, enlisted personnel with less than two years of experience earned between $13,656 and $21,800, including base pay and a typical food allotment and housing allowance. (There is additional pay for serving in high-cost-of-living areas and hazardous duty assignments.) Enlisted men with ten years of service earned between $13,656 and $33,072. Officers earn significantly more. Those with less than two years of service — known in the Army, Air Force, and Marines as second lieutenants and in the Navy and Coast Guard as ensigns — earn between $21,850 and $79,018. Officers with ten years' experience can earn as much as $85,986 as admirals, with captains earning nearly $50,000.

How does one go about signing up for the military? What determines which branch of the service is right for you?

The five military services — Army, Navy, Air Force, Marine Corps, and Coast Guard — hire nearly half a million young men and women each year. Collectively, the services offer training and jobs in 134 military occupations. According to Don Betterton in *How the Military Will Help You Pay for College,* "The five military services . . . are looking for the same type of person: a man or woman aged seventeen to thirty-five who is a United States citizen or permanent resident, in good physical condition, of good moral character, and motivated to serve his or her country. A high school diploma, although not an absolute requirement, is highly recommended. [Currently about 90 percent of enlistees have graduated from high school.] All enlistees must also meet minimum standards on a military aptitude test."

If you are considering joining the military, your first step should be to see your local recruiter. If you aren't sure which branch you'd like to join, go to the recruiting office of each of the branches in which you're interested and ask what they have to offer you. Most likely, each recruiter will insist that his or her branch has the most to offer, so it's important that you go in knowing what you want to get out of the military. William Colon Sr., a retired Air Force sergeant who teaches aerospace science and is affiliated with the junior ROTC program at Cherry Hill High School West in Cherry Hill, New Jersey, says, "Choosing a branch of the military is a very individual decision. It's like shopping — you familiarize yourself with the choices and you make a decision on what you want, based on what's best for you."

After you have made your choice, you will be asked to report to a processing center where you will take a medical exam and a series of aptitude tests. Based on those results, as well as on your level of education, you will receive a regular assignment or qualify for a special program. A typical enlistment is for three to six years. You will be asked to sign an enlistment contract which states that, in return for your services for a certain period of time, the military will provide you with a job and a salary.

Do you think America should reinstate the draft?

"I really don't think the draft should be reinstituted. I feel strongly that the United States has enough troops in the Middle East right now. If the war goes on for a long time then it is a different story because we will have no other choice but to have the draft." —*Mary, a ninth grader from Chicago, Illinois*

"I really don't want the draft to start because I have an older brother that just turned nineteen years old and I'm afraid that he will get drafted." —*Vanessa, a ninth grader from Nashville, Tennessee*

"My feeling toward the draft is that as long as the United States is doing well, there will be no draft. If we start losing the war then I feel the draft should definitely be reinstated." —*Suzanne, an eleventh grader from Killen, Alabama*

"I feel they should definitely reinstitute the draft because soon the United States will run out of soldiers." —*Jennifer, an eleventh grader from Pierre, South Dakota*

"The draft should definitely not be reinstated. If it does get reinstated then the United States has gone too far in this war. I am totally against the draft." —*Patricia, a tenth grader from Towson, Maryland*

TEENSPEAK:

What do you think is going to happen when the war in the Gulf is over?

"I think when the war is over it's going to leave Saddam's people very angry towards the United States. I definitely think things will quiet down over there. I really think Saddam will be overthrown by his people, and if they don't do it, we will. The new government that will replace Saddam will be much more democratic; that is, if the United States ends up winning." —*Poornima, a ninth grader from Scarsdale, New York*

"I think Saddam is going to be overthrown by the United States. I think Iraq will have a much more democratic government. As the war is, I think we will be in debt and they will be in debt, but our country won't gain anything from the war. I think the war will be forgotten and we will establish peace treaties with the Iraqis." —*Meredyth, a tenth grader from North Miami Beach, Florida*

"I think the war is going to be ended by the U.S. bombing Iraq. Saddam will realize we are more powerful than him. Even if Saddam dies, I think there are plenty of people with Saddam who can take over. He is going to die a hero. He will die for his country. I don't think Iraq is going to be totally free. People are afraid to say what they think. Iraq may stop taking over other countries, but it won't be as democratic as people would like it to be." —*Christine, a twelfth grader from Glen Cove, New York*

"First of all, I think Israel is going to get involved. The United States will eventually win. I also think the war will go on for a long time. There is going to be a ground war. Saddam is not giving up so fast. I really think his people are going to realize what he is doing and possibly overrule him. I think that after the war, the United States will do what we did in Japan. We'll set up an economy and government that will be much more democratic. I think Kuwait will remain on its own, but the United States will have to step in and help them get back on their feet." —*Lauren, an eighth grader from Newark, New Jersey*

"I think the war will end by Saddam pulling out of Kuwait. I think the United States will intervene and start a government like we did in Panama. We will restore Kuwait to its original state, but we will restrict Iraq like we did Germany after World War I. I don't think the United States will settle for anything less than that. It will definitely be much more democratic since Saddam will not pull out for a long time, so the emotions of the people will have been tortured for so long that they'll want democracy." —*Leo, a tenth grader from Teaneck, New Jersey*

"I really think the war will end by the United States overthrowing Saddam. When the war is over, Kuwait will run its own country, with the United States helping them to get back on their feet. I don't think that the U.S. will help Iraq run their country, because the Iraqis will want to run it. I don't think the United States will leave until peace treaties have been made. Iraq will never have the same kind of government as the United States." —*Caroline, a ninth grader from New York, New York*

"I think the United States will remove Iraq from Kuwait. Eventually, Iraq will surrender, and the United States will be in control of what happens and will reconstruct Iraq. I think the United States will completely control Iraq. They want to prevent this from happening again. The United States will help Kuwait get its feet back on the ground because it is such an important country to us and the U.S. has supported them all along. I imagine Iraq will be more democratic because they will learn from their mistakes. They will realize that having a dictator can really hurt the country." —*Gregg, a twelfth grader from Mendota Heights, Minnesota*

"I think the United States will definitely win the war. In order for the war to be over, we are going to have to kill Hussein. Once he is dead, the United States will take over the territory or let the Iraqi people run their own country. At that time, the people will want to run a democratic country like the United States. I think Kuwait will stay the same by remaining free." —*Ricky, a seventh grader from Tenafly, New Jersey*

"I think the Kuwaiti government will return to power. In Iraq the government will depend on whether Hussein is still alive and what power he will be given and how his people will react to him. I have a feeling one man will remain in power in Iraq, but a replacement will be made. I hope the U.S. does not try to take over and help the government, because it will cause more problems."
—*Curt, a twelfth grader from Wilmington, Delaware*

Afterword

An End to War

"Some generation of mankind was eventually bound to face the task of abolishing war, because civilization was bound to endow us sooner or later with the power to destroy ourselves. We happen to be that generation, though we do not ask for the honor and do not feel ready for it. There is nobody wiser who will take the responsibility and solve this problem for us. We have to it ourselves."
—Gwynne Dyer, *War*

Okay, so now some of your questions about the situation in the Middle East, specifically the Persian Gulf, have been answered. You have a better understanding of the context in which we've gone to war. But how can you relax and start to worry about the simple things — grades, extracurricular activities, part-time jobs, post–high school plans, friends, romance — when our nation is engaged in a potentially devastating conflict that seems to have no solution in sight? Even victory for the Allied forces would be bittersweet. There will have been many casualties, including men, women, and children; the environment already has sustained extensive damage; and your generation — and, perhaps, many generations to come — will be left trying to close the wounds of a war that may have implications beyond anything we could have imagined.

Today's teenagers have been termed "realists," pragmatic idealists who refuse to wait for the reins of power to be turned over to them. Instead, high school students around the country have made a commitment to act now, to get a head start on solving the problems that threaten to overwhelm our world as we head toward the new millennium.

This past summer and fall, we asked thousands of teenagers to share their concerns about the real world. Most of you responded to our questions at least a few weeks before tensions in the Gulf escalated into a fullscale war. Still, you can see from the remarks included here that teens were already keenly aware of the heavy burden that has been placed upon their shoulders.

"I worry about war in the Middle East, hunger in Russia, environmental concerns, homelessness in the United States, drugs, and gang violence." —Chris, a twelfth grader from Coon Rapids, Minnesota

"World peace worries me and having our generation have to rebuild the entire world — economically, environmentally, and socially." —Mieka, a tenth grader from Washington, D.C.

"I worry that the very real problems that our society faces will become secondary to the need to succeed and get ahead." —Matt, a twelfth grader from Rutland, Vermont

"I worry that America is falling as a world power, due to the social and economic strains that have occurred in the past twenty years." —Michael, a tenth grader from Naperville, Illinois

"What worries me about the real world is what is happening at the present time. People are fighting, and hunger is very abundant. It worries me that if nothing can be done now, how are we going to help it in the future?" —Doug, a twelfth grader from Fairbanks, Alaska

"I am worried that the Middle East crisis may get worse. I also see people being less kind to each other. Many people are only interested in themselves. A world filled with selfish people is not exciting to me." —*Ben, an eleventh grader from Honolulu, Hawaii*

"The attitudes of some people scare me. It seems that everyone is looking out for themselves but more and more often they overlook other people's problems and don't care how they could help other people. Just how people treat their fellow citizens in general is scary. It appears that people don't have feelings for anyone but themselves." —*Katy, a tenth grader from La Jolla, California*

"I worry about not having the chance to live my dream because of all the many problems that I am seeing every day. War, crime, and an absence of opportunity are my top three worries."—*Karen, a tenth grader from Abbeville, Alabama*

"I worry about the condition of how our country will be in relation to other countries. The idea of having to provide for myself and my family and all the responsibilities that follow worry me. What the economic conditions of our country will be concerns me." —*Aaron, an eleventh grader from Grapevine, Texas*

"What worries me about the real world are the drugs and world hunger, and how children and senior citizens around the world are mistreated." —*Kari, a ninth grader from Fairbanks, Alaska*

"I am worried by the idea of war. I would like to live in a more peaceful world. I am also greatly concerned about the number of homeless people." —*Felicia, an eleventh grader from La Jolla, California*

"I worry about racism, insidious racism born of fear and passed from generation to generation through ignorance. This is the hardest racism to fight because it is outside the law. I worry about scores of people stuck in an educational rut and unable to lead a decent life — hence, illiteracy, drug abuse, and gangs. I fear nations blinded by propaganda, taught to hate others and covet war. I see the abuse of our environment. I see the abuse of human rights throughout the world. I fear these things; I fear that an anti-utopia may raise its ugly head while we aren't looking."—*Sarah, a twelfth grader from Grosse Pointe, Michigan*

Not too many years ago, American teens were accused of selfishness and apathy — of total unconcern for the people around them. Teens in the nineties have proven otherwise. You have shown yourselves to be committed to positive action and change. You've started schoolwide and communitywide recycling programs. You've worked to put an end to drunk driving. You've raised funds to house the homeless and feed the hungry. You've pressured our leaders to commit more funds to AIDS research.

Now you're faced with perhaps the greatest challenge. For the first time in your lives, war is not an abstraction — a battle fought between faceless, nameless combatants on a field far, far away. The war in the Persian Gulf has touched us all. Many of you have a father or mother, sister or brother in the Gulf. Others have friends among the troops. In one way or another, we all are affected when Americans go to war.

If any good can come out of this war, perhaps it is this: a renewed commitment to peace, a commitment to ensure that future generations need not suffer the horrors of armed conflict; a commitment by your generation — the next generation of leaders — to find peaceful solutions to our global problems. Only then can we hope to protect our planet from further harm and work together with all the nations on Earth to ensure a free and just future for us all.

America at War

Wars and Other Military Actions Involving the United States

• 1812–1815   **War of 1812**

The net result of this war between the United States and Great Britain was a draw. The Treaty of Ghent, signed in Belgium in 1814, provided for all captured land to be returned. The issues that led to the conflict — trade embargos, British support of the American Indians (which inhibited U.S. expansion), and the impressment of British-born sailors aboard U.S. ships — were never resolved.

• 1846–1848   **Mexican War**

The immediate cause of the war was the U.S. annexation of Texas (then an independent republic) and the American desire to expand. The Treaty of Guadalupe Hidalgo ended the war, with a cost to Mexico of two-fifths of its territory and a cost to the United States of $15 million.

• 1861–1865   **Civil War**

Twenty-three states from the North — the Union — fought against eleven

Southern states, a.k.a. the Confederacy. The key issues that divided the two halves of America: the expansion of slavery to new states; states' rights versus Federal authority; the abolitionist movement; and sectional rivalry. The Union won, and slavery was abolished.

• 1898   **Spanish-American War**
The United States and Spain went to war largely because the United States supported Cuban independence from Spain. The Treaty of Paris ended Spanish rule in Cuba. The United States gained the islands of Guam, Puerto Rico, and the Philippines.

• 1914–1918   **World War I** (United States entered in 1917)
The first world war was fought in France, Belgium, Germany, Italy, and Russia. The primary combatants were the "Central Powers" — Germany, Austria-Hungary, and Turkey — and the "Allies" — Britain, France, Russia, and the United States. This was the first conflict that America entered to defend democracy, although the deaths of 128 Americans aboard the *Lusitania* in 1915 and unrestricted German submarine warfare also played a major role in the U.S. decision to enter the conflict. World War I, which the Allies won resoundingly, set the stage for World War II and also helped to topple the emperors of Austria-Hungary, Germany, and Russia.

• 1939–1945   **World War II** (United States entered in 1941)
The U.S. joined the Allies (chiefly Great Britain and the Soviet Union) against the Axis Powers (Germany, Italy, and Japan) after Japan attacked Pearl Harbor. A few days later, Germany and Italy declared war on the United States. Ultimately, the United States and the Soviet Union emerged as the strongest countries in the world, and the Soviet Union cut itself off from noncommunist countries and began to take control of Eastern Europe. At the end of World War II, the United Nations was formed — to prevent future world wars.

• 1950–1953   **Korean War**
Following the North Korean invasion of South Korea, forces of the United Nations (primarily the United States and South Korea) fought North Korea and, eventually, communist China. Technically this was not a war — rather, President Truman committed the United States to what he termed "a police action." The war ended as a stalemate, and the demilitarized

zone, established by an armistice signed by the United States and North Korea, still separates the two hostile countries.

•1957–1975   **Vietnam War** (U.S. troops involved 1964–1973)
The war in Vietnam was fought between South Vietnam, aided by the United States, and the communist guerrilla insurgents (Vietcong), backed by North Vietnam. War was never declared by the United States, but the Gulf of Tonkin Resolution (1964) authorized U.S. involvement. By 1969, United States troops numbered approximately 550,000.

Since the end of the Vietnam War in 1975, the United States has undertaken two armed interventions: **Grenada** in 1983 and **Panama** in 1989.
    The United States has also been involved in several other military actions since that time. These actions have taken place in the following areas:

- **Iran** in 1980 (mission to rescue American hostages);
- **Sinai, Egypt,** in 1982 (the United States was a member of a multinational peacekeeping force);
- **Lebanon** in 1982–1983 (U.S. Marines participated in the multinational force that aided the Lebanese government);
- **Libya** in 1986 (the United States bombed Tripoli in retaliation for alleged terrorist activities);
- **Persian Gulf** in 1987–1988 (during the Iran-Iraq War, the U.S. Navy escorted Kuwaiti oil tankers through the Gulf);
- **Philippines** in 1989 (the United States sent fighter pilots to assist the Philippine government during a coup attempt); and
- **Saudi Arabia** since 1990.

In addition, U.S. military advisers have been sent abroad to a number of overseas locations, including **El Salvador,** from 1981 to the present; **Honduras**, from 1983 to 1989; **Chad** in 1983; and **Bolivia, Columbia,** and **Peru,** from 1989 to the present.

The War in the Gulf

Week One

January 16 U.S., British, Saudi, and Kuwaiti warplanes and cruise missiles undertake a massive air assualt against targets in Iraq and Kuwait. Initial targets are reportedly Iraqi missile sites; chemical, biological, and nuclear weapons production facilities; and other military targets. Iraqi response is minimal, and Allied losses are few.

January 17 Eight to ten Iraqi Scud missiles hit Tel Aviv and Haifa in Israel, but no more than 20 civilians are wounded, and none are killed. The Iraqi missiles carried conventional (not chemical or biological) warheads. The Israeli government publicly and forcefully reserves the right to respond but has yet to indicate what its response will be. The U.S. and Allied air assault continues on Iraq and Kuwait, with reports of fewer than ten U.S. and Allied planes downed. In the first 30 hours of attack, more than 2,000 Allied aerial missions (or "sorties") are undertaken.

January 18 Turkish assembly approves U.S. use of airbases; PLO and Jordan condemn attack on Iraq.

January 19 To defend against Iraqi Scud attacks, the United States supplies Israel with Patriot anti-missile systems, operated by U.S. crews, in Israel.

January 20 U.S. Commander General H. Norman Schwarzkopf says that Allied bombers have "thoroughly damaged" Iraqi nuclear research reactors. Iraq launches first Scuds toward Saudi Arabia; most or all are intercepted by U.S. Patriot missiles. No Scuds hit Israel. Saddam Hussein asks other Arabs to join in a holy war (*jihad*) against the Allied forces.

January 21 Allied officials reassess earlier claims of air superiority over Iraq in light of continuing Scud missile counterattacks. U.S. Defense Secretary Cheney says war "could conceivably be weeks, could conceivably be months." Citing civilian casualties from Allied bombing, the Iraqi military announces plans to "distribute . . . more than 20 prisoners [captured Allied airmen] among scientific and economic targets." Stating that such "distribution" would violate the Geneva convention on the treatment of prisoners, the International Red Cross cautions Iraq about such action.

January 22 Tel Aviv suburb hit by Iraqi Scud missile; Israeli military says three people are killed and seventy wounded. Iraq sets fire to two Kuwaiti oil refineries and an oil field, as Saddam Hussein had earlier threatened it would if his occupation of Kuwait were challenged.

January 23 After one week of war, President Bush says "Operation Desert Storm is right on schedule." Japan announces decision to increase financial support for Allied effort by $9 billion. Israeli officials say their government will not launch an immediate retaliatory strike against Iraq, despite Tuesday's deadly attack on Tel Aviv.

(Sources: *New York Times, Washington Post, Middle East Report, Israel & Palestine Political Report*, compiled by ACCESS: A Security Information Service, and published as *ACCESS Guide to the Persian Gulf Crisis* — Updated Edition)

Read All About It

Current Books on the Persian Gulf

A Concise History of the Middle East by Arthur Goldschmidt (Westview Press, 1987)

From Beirut to Jerusalem by Thomas Friedman (Anchor Press, 1989)

"The Middle East: New Frictions, New Alignments." *Great Decisions*, New York, Foreign Policy Association, 1991

Middle East Patterns: Places, Peoples, and Politics by Colbert C. Held (Westview Press, 1989)

The Modern History of Iraq by Phebe Marr (Westview Press, 1985)

Palestine and the Arab-Israeli Conflict by Charles D. Smith (St. Martin's Press, 1988)

The Persian Gulf States: A General Survey by Alvin J. Cottrell (The Johns Hopkins University Press, 1980)

The Rape of Kuwait by Jean P. Sasson (Knightsbridge Publishing, 1991)

Republic of Fear: The Politics of Modern Iraq by Samir al-Khalil (Pantheon Books, 1989)

War by Gwynne Dyer (Crown, 1985)

Hungry for Information?

A Guide to Organizations in the Know

The following organizations can provide you with information on policies, positions, and resources regarding war and peace in the Persian Gulf and throughout the Middle East.

ACCESS: A Security Information Service
1730 M Street, N.W., Suite 605
Washington, DC 20036
(202) 785-6630

Alliance for Our Common Future
c/o National Peace Institute Foundation
110 Maryland Avenue, N.E.
Washington, DC 20003
(202) 546-9500

American-Arab Affairs Council
1730 K Street, N.W., Suite 512
Washington, DC 20036
(202) 296-6767

American-Arab Anti-Discrimination
    Committee
4201 Connecticut Avenue, N.W., Suite 500
Washington, DC 20008
(202) 244-2990

American Association for the Advancement
    of Science — Program on Science and
    International Security
1333 H Street, N.W.
Washington, DC 20005
(202) 326-6490

American Civil Liberties Union
122 Maryland Avenue, N.E.
Washington, DC 20002
(202) 544-1681

American Committee on US–Soviet Relations
109 11th Street, S.E.
Washington, DC 20003
(202) 546-1700

American Educational Trust
P.O. Box 53062
Washington, DC 20009
(202) 939-6050

American Friends Service Committee
Middle East Peace Education Program
1501 Cherry Street
Philadelphia, PA 19102
(215) 241-7019

American Israel Public Affairs Committee
440 First Street, S.W., Suite 600
Washington, DC 20001
(202) 639-5200

Americans for Middle East Understanding
475 Riverside Drive, Room 771
New York, NY 10115
(212) 870-2146

Amnesty International
322 Eighth Avenue
New York, NY 10001
(212) 807-8400

Arab American Institute
918 16th Street, N.W., Suite 601
Washington, DC 20006
(202) 429-9210

Arms Control Association
11 Dupont Circle, N.W.
Washington, DC 20036
(202) 797-4626

Brookings Institution
Foreign Policy Studies Program
1775 Massachusetts Avenue, N.W.
Washington, DC 20036
(202) 797-6010

Campaign for Peace and Democracy
P.O. Box 1640, Cathedral Station
New York, NY 10025
(212) 666-5924

Carnegie Endowment for International Peace
2400 N Street, N.W.
Washington, DC 20037-1118
(202) 862-7900

Carter Center of Emory University
One Copenhill
Atlanta, GA 30307
(404) 420-5117

Cato Institute
224 Second Street, S.E.
Washington, DC 20003
(202) 546-0200

Center for Defense Information
1500 Massachusetts Avenue, N.W.
Washington, DC 20005
(202) 862-0700

Center for Innovative Diplomacy
17931-F Sky Park Circle
Irvine, CA 92714
(714) 250-1296

Center for Strategic and International
   Studies
1800 K Street, N.W., Suite 400
Washington, DC 20006
(202) 887-0200

Citizens for a Free Kuwait
P.O. Box 21
Falls Church, VA 22040
(202) 364-2232

Coalition for America at Risk
c/o Keene, Shirley & Associates
919 Prince Street
Alexandria, VA 22314
(703) 684-0550

Coalition to Stop U.S. Intervention in the
    Middle East
36 East 12th Street
New York, NY 10003
(212) 546-0200

Committee for Peace and Security in the Gulf
2300 M Street, N.W., Suite 600
Washington, DC 20037
(202) 293-1525

Common Cause
2030 M Street, N.W.
Washington, DC 20036
(202) 833-1200

Council on Foreign Relations
58 East 68th Street
New York, NY 10021
(212) 734-0400

Fellowship of Reconciliation
P.O. Box 271, 523 North Broadway
Nyack, NY 10960
(914) 358-4601

Foreign Policy Association
729 Seventh Avenue
New York, NY 10019
(212) 764-4050

Foreign Policy Research Institute
3615 Chestnut Street
Philadelphia, PA 19104
(215) 382-0685

Georgetown University
Center for Contemporary Arab Studies
501 Intercultural Center
Washington, DC 20057
(202) 687-5793

George Washington University
Security Policy Studies Program
Elliott School of International Affairs
Washington, DC 20052
(202) 994-6425

Heritage Foundation
214 Massachusetts Avenue, N.W.
Washington, DC 20002
(202) 546-4400

Institute for Foreign Policy Analysis
675 Massachusetts Avenue, 10th Floor
Cambridge, MA 02139
(617) 492-2116

Institute for International Economics
11 Dupont Circle, N.W.
Washington, DC 20036
(202) 328-9000

Institute for Policy Studies
1601 Connecticut Avenue, N.W., 5th Floor
Washington, DC 20009
(202) 234-9382

International Security Council
1155 15th Street, N.W., Suite 502
Washington, DC 20005
(202) 828-0802

Jewish Institute for National Security Affairs
1100 17th Street, N.W., Suite 330
Washington, DC 20036
(202) 833-0020

Jobs with Peace Campaign
76 Summer Street
Boston, MA 02110
(617) 338-5783

Johns Hopkins University
Paul H. Nitze School of Advanced International Studies
1740 Massachusetts Avenue, N.W.
Washington, DC 20036
(202) 663-5600

League of Arab States — Palestine Affairs
   Center
1730 K Street, N.W., Suite 703
Washington, DC 20006
(202) 785-8394

League of Women Voters
1730 M Street, N.W.
Washington, DC 20036
(202) 429-1965

Middle East Institute
1761 N Street, N.W.
Washington, DC 20036
(202) 785-1141

Middle East Research and Information
   Project
1500 Massachusetts Avenue, N.W., Suite 119
Washington, DC 20005
(202) 223-3677

Middle East Studies Association of North
   America
University of Arizona
1232 North Cherry Avenue
Tucson, AZ 85721
(602) 621-5850

Military Families Support Network
122 Maryland Avenue, N.E.
Washington, DC 20002
(202) 543-0974

Mobilization for Survival
45 John Street, Suite 811
New York, NY 10038
(212) 385-2222

National Association of Arab Americans
2033 M Street, N.W., Suite 300
Washington, DC 20036-3399
(202) 467-4800

National Campaign for Peace in the Middle
   East
104 Fulton Street, Room 303
New York, NY 10038
(212) 227-0221

National Council of the Churches of Christ in
   the U.S.A.
110 Maryland Avenue, N.E.
Washington, DC 20002
(202) 544-2350

National Council on U.S.–Arab Relations
1735 I Street, N.W., Suite 515
Washington, DC 20036
(202) 293-0801

National Peace Institute Foundation
110 Maryland Avenue, N.E.
Washington, DC 20002
(202) 546-9500

National US–Arab Chamber of Commerce
1825 K Street, N.W., Suite 1107
Washington, DC 20006
(202) 331-8010

Nuclear Age Peace Foundation
1187 Coast Village Road, Suite 123
Santa Barbara, CA 93108
(805) 965-3443

Nuclear Control Institute
1000 Connecticut Avenue, N.W., Suite 704
Washington, DC 20036
(202) 822-8444

Ohio State University
 Mershon Center
199 West 10th Avenue
Columbus, OH 43201-2399
(614) 292-1681

Operation Real Security
2076 East Alameda Drive
Tempe, AZ 85282
(602) 921-3090

OPTIONS: A University Outreach Project on
 International Security
Brown University
131 Waterman Street
Providence, RI 02901
(401) 331-4626

Professionals' Coalition for Nuclear Arms
 Control
1616 P Street, N.W., Suite 320
Washington, DC 20036
(202) 332-4823

Psychologists for Social Responsibility
1841 Columbia Road, N.W., Suite 207
Washington, DC 20009
(202) 745-7084

Stanford University
Hoover Institute
Stanford, CA 94305
(415) 723-1754

Study Circles Resource Center
Route 169, P.O. Box 203
Pomfret, CT 06258
(203) 928-2616

Third World Resources
464 19th Street
Oakland, CA 94612-9761
(415) 835-4692

20/20 Vision
1000 16th Street, N.W., Suite 810
Washington, DC 20036
(202) 728-1157

United Church of Christ
110 Maryland Avenue, N.E.
Washington, DC 20002
(202) 543-1517

United Nations Association of the United
 States of America
485 Fifth Avenue
New York, NY 10017
(212) 697-3232

United States Catholic Conference
3211 Fourth Street, N.E.
Washington, DC 20017-1194
(202) 541-3000

United States Institute of Peace
1550 M Street, N.W., Suite 700
Washington, DC 20005
(202) 457-1700

University of California at Berkeley
Institute of International Studies
215 Moses Hall
Berkeley, CA 94720
(415) 642-2472

Washington Institute for Near East Policy
1828 L Street, N.W., Suite 1050
Washington, DC 20036
(202) 452-0650

Winston Foundation for World Peace
401 Commonwealth Avenue
Boston, MA 02215
(617) 266-1193

About the Authors

Marian Salzman is the author of six books, including *Greetings from High School* and *150 Ways Teens Can Make a Difference*, both for Peterson's Guides, and *Wanted: Liberal Arts Graduates* (Doubleday, 1987). She is managing director of the editorial services/marketing communications firm The Bedford Kent Group, of New York City and London. Salzman is a graduate of Brown University, Class of 1981, and River Dell Regional High School in Oradell, New Jersey, and has been editor in chief of *CV: The College Magazine* and *bc* (Before College) magazine. She has also been editor of *Management Review* magazine, and her writing credits include *Forbes*, *Ms.*, and *Self*. She has been featured in dozens of newspapers and magazines, including *Business Week*, *Glamour*, the *New York Times*, the *New York Daily News*, *Savvy*, and *Womens' Wear Daily*, and she is a regular guest on radio and television.

    Ann O'Reilly is a freelance editor and writer based in Washington state. She is co-author of three books in the "Peterson's H.S." series. She has been senior editor and copy chief of *CV: The College Magazine* and *bc* (Before College) magazine. Ann is a graduate of Bowdoin College, Class of 1984, and the University of Denver Publishing Institute, Class of 1986. She grew up in New York City and Pelham Manor, New York, and is a graduate of The Ethel Walker School in Simsbury, Connecticut.

Teresa Reisgies is an assistant editor at The Bedford Kent Group and a graduate of Georgetown University, Class of 1989. She is also co-author of *Greetings from High School* and *150 Ways Teens Can Make a Difference.* Teresa grew up in Alpine, New Jersey, and is a graduate of Tenafly High School in Tenafly, New Jersey. She lives in New York City.

Terry Lynn Barnett manages media and school relations for The Bedford Kent Group. She grew up in Bethesda, Maryland; graduated from Walt Whitman High School in Bethesda; and earned a B.S. from Syracuse University in 1988.

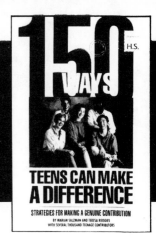